AMID MY QUESTIONABLE EXISTENCE

HOPE, FAITH, PURPOSE, AND DREAMS

RACHEL TUGUTU

Copyright © 2024 Rachel Tugutu

All rights reserved.

ISBN: 9786586354393

DEDICATION

"Before I formed you in the womb, I knew you; Before you were born, I sanctified you.
I ordained you a prophet to the nations."

— Jeremiah 1:5 New King James Version (NKJV).

Table of Contents

PROLOGUE *4*

CHAPTER 1 .... *21*

   SHE IS INCOMPARABLE 21

CHAPTER 2 .... *93*

   ONE STEP AT A TIME: WORKING TO UNDERSTAND A CLEAR BIG PICTURE OF WHAT TO DO NEXT 93

CHAPTER 3 .... *128*

   WHAT IS MY CALLING? IS IT THE ONE? 128

CHAPTER 4 .... *164*

   THE DEBUT OF MY FIRST ALBUM . 164

CHAPTER 5 .... *195*

   A NEW DIFFERENT WORLD 195

CHAPTER 6 .... *382*

THE YEAR I SURRENDERED MY LIFE TO GOD: TIRED OF LIVING MY WAY 382

CHAPTER 7 .... *426*

LONGING FOR PEACE AND COMFORT: LETTING GOD TAKE CONTROL OF MY LIFE 426

CHAPTER 8 .... *483*

A NEW PROFOUND MINDSET: SEEING THINGS THROUGH THE LENS OF GOD 483

CHAPTER 9 .... *517*

UNEXPECTED EVENTS 517

PROLOGUE

As a middle school student, I found solace under the shade of a magnificent tree as the afternoon sun casts a golden glow upon the schoolyard. The sound of giggling students filled the air as I sat, deep in thought. Just as my worries threatened to overwhelm me, a melodious voice resonated through my ears, prompting me to look up.

"Hey, is everything okay?"

AMID MY QUESTIONABLE EXISTENCE

Turning my gaze toward the source of the voice, I was taken aback by seeing my teacher approaching me with a warm smile. A flicker of surprise danced in my eyes before I mustered the courage to respond.

"Uh, yeah, I guess so," I mumbled, my voice barely above a whisper.

The teacher gracefully settled down beside me, our eyes meeting in genuine concern. With a gentle pat on the back, we began to speak words that carried the weight of a thousand possibilities.

"You've got a bright future ahead of you, my dear student," the teacher said, our voice filled with pride and hope.

The sparse words resonated deep within my heart, causing a burst of inspiration to flood my weary soul. My eyes lit up with newfound determination as I whispered, "Really? You think so?"

The teacher nodded; our eyes filled with certainty. "Absolutely. You have incredible potential."

I felt a surge of gratitude towards the teacher who believed in me. Her encouragement ignited a fire within me, dispelling the clouds of doubt that had plagued my mind.

I squared my shoulders with renewed purpose and declared, "Thank you, teacher. I won't let you down."

The teacher grinned; our smile was radiant with conviction. "I know you won't. Now, let's go and make your dreams a reality."

And with that, our journey towards a bright future began.

In the shimmering warmth of that Thursday afternoon, a teacher's words became the guiding light for me, setting the stage for an incredible journey of growth and self-discovery.

And so, our story began.

As the school bell rang, signaling the start of the afternoon break, I was hesitating near the girls, chatting animatedly by the old oak tree. Taking a deep breath, I mustered up all the courage I could find and walked towards them.

"Um," I stammered, hoping to catch their attention.

The girls glanced at me, their conversations tapering off into curiosity-filled silence. One of them, with vibrant pink hair, raised an eyebrow and prompted, "What's up?"

Summoning every ounce of determination, I blurted out, "Can I join you girls?"

There was a brief pause, their expressions shifting between surprise and amusement. The girl with the light-dark hair smiled mischievously before replying, "Sure thing! The more the merrier, right?"

Relief washed over me as I stepped into their circle, grateful for the opportunity to step out of my comfort zone. The other girls greeted me warmly, making me feel instantly at ease.

One of them, a girl with a contagious giggle, nudged me playfully. "You're brave for approaching us, you know. What made you want to join?"

I took a deep breath, allowing my vulnerability to show. "I'm tired of being alone. I want to make more friends and experience new things."

The girls shared knowing glances and nodded in understanding. The vibrant brown-haired girl, as one of the girls said, "Well, you've come to the right group. We'll help you escape that shell, one crazy adventure at a time!"

And just like that, my journey to step out of my comfort zone began, filled with laughter, shared secrets, and unexpected friendships.

I kept telling myself, but I would always end up alone again!

The next day, a teacher approached me again during class break. "Hey, young girl, is everything okay?" asked one of the schoolteachers passing by. And I only responded with a smile on my face.

I had always been an outcast in school. The other kids recognized that I was different—that I didn't have the same confidence and ease in social situations as I did. I was constantly tripping over my words, saying the wrong thing, or having difficulty fitting in. The other kids weren't particularly mean to me, but they never truly accepted me either.

Despite my anxieties and social awkwardness, I loved having friends and being part of a group. I dreamed of belonging somewhere, being accepted, and being able to relate to others meaningfully.

Regarding playtime, I would stay alone or play imaginary games with my stones or small wooden sticks, reciting stories in my head. I was a wonderful storyteller with plenty of imagination, but there wasn't anyone around to appreciate my tales.

As a little girl with a reserved personality, I often felt like those around me misunderstood me. I took my natural inclination to spend more time alone than with a crowd as a sign that I wasn't friendly or didn't want to be part of the group. I was teased throughout the school for not joining in with activities or conversations as much as the other students, which only further alienated me from them.

But the truth was that I did enjoy spending time with people; I just kept my guard up because I feared being judged. Finding the courage to open up and share my thoughts and feelings took me a long time. I was afraid the truth of who I was wouldn't be accepted, and I'd be rejected again.

When I finally did open, I was surprised that many of my peers felt the same. We had all been hiding in our shells, afraid to be seen. Our group quickly became a haven, and it was refreshing to be accepted finally.

Slowly, I started to understand that the person I was on the inside wasn't any different than who I was on the outside. I began to accept and embrace my personality, knowing that while it may still cause some misunderstandings, it also made me unique.

I knew that feeling misunderstood, judged, and outcasted was part of growing up and that I must endure to find my proper place in the world. I knew that some would never understand me and that that was okay. But I also knew that if I could embrace my uniqueness and be myself, I would be accepted for who I was, and that was worth any ridicule or judgment.

My faith brought me a newfound happiness and contentment I had never felt before. I finally felt confident that I was making the right choices and living the right way. Even when life got tough, I believed God should be at the center of our lives.

***

My family and I joined together to put God at the center of our lives. I'd bring my friends to church services and joyfully lead a bible study at home. I was a light in my community, and I believed that, through my faith, I could make the world a better place.

As a young girl with a strong faith, I believed that the key to a good life was to put God first in every area of my life, decision, or everything. I thought that if I stayed on the path of God, then He would give me the guidance I needed to lead a fulfilling life.

I dedicated my life to following the path of God, no matter how hard it seemed. I prayed regularly and read the Bible regularly. I also lived a life of service. I donated my time, energy, and money to local ministries and charities.

AMID MY QUESTIONABLE EXISTENCE

I was a reticent and introverted girl in school. I was often the subject of ridicule by my peers. I always sat in the back of the class and sometimes at the front, not speaking up but quietly taking everything in. Every day, I felt like an outsider, looking at a world I did not understand.

I continued to put God first in all aspects of my life faithfully. I had a deeper understanding of what it means to trust in God and His plan for my life. I understand that no matter what surprises and hardships life brings, God is always with me and wants nothing more than for me to succeed.

As the sun hung low in the sky, I went down the city's bustling streets. The school had ended for the day, and I relished the freedom from the monotony of textbooks and lectures. In these cherished moments of solitude, I found myself lost in thought, my mind wandering through the possibilities that lay before me.

As I walked, a vibrant melody floated through the air, increasing in volume with every step. Intrigued, Emily turned a corner, and I found myself face to face with a street musician, her fingers dancing across her guitar strings. A smile tugged at my lips as the woman strummed with a passion that resonated within her.

"Isn't it incredible how music can stir something deep within us?" the woman said, her voice carrying a touch of whimsy. I couldn't help but nod in agreement.

"It's like a language that speaks straight to our hearts," I responded, my eyes never leaving the musician's nimble fingers.

The woman grinned, her eyes lighting up. "You have a soul that yearns to create, my dear. Never forget that. You're destined for greatness."

My heart skipped a beat, the words sinking deep into my core. I had always felt a spark within me, an urge to tell stories and weave worlds with my words. But doubt had always loomed, casting shadows over my dreams.

"Thank you," I whispered, my voice filled with determination.

The musician's laughter twinkled like falling stars, and she plucked a few final notes before bidding me farewell. "Remember, my dear, everything happens for a reason. Your journey starts now."

And with those words, I watched the woman disappear into the crowd, leaving me with a renewed sense of purpose.

Filled with excitement and inspiration, I quickened my pace, my mind buzzing with possibilities. A story was beginning to take shape within me, eager to be released onto the pages of my imagination.

Ready to embrace the greatness that awaited me, I stepped forward, my heart alight with the fire of creativity. This was just the beginning, and I was determined to seize the adventure.

PART ONE

CHAPTER 1

SHE IS INCOMPARABLE

I was born in Shinyanga Region in August of 1998. Located in Tanzania. The region is known for its diamonds, gold, and livestock, keeping with rich culture and tradition.

I had been close to my family since I was a little girl, and the time I spent in my hometown of Shinyanga, Tanzania, was no different. I spent all my childhood days with my parents and sisters, never missing an opportunity to bond with them.

But I loved one thing more than anything– exploring the city and its many hidden spots. To me, Shinyanga was like a treasure chest. I often became lost in the winding roads and narrow alleys, taking in the sights and sounds of the bustling town.

I would take the time to explore different areas where we currently reside with my siblings and other children, participating in friendly debates about the best spot to watch the sunrises or play. I loved discovering new places; its remarkable and unique culture greatly impacted me.

But at the same time, the city also had its share of difficulties. Even though tangible beauty like fresh produce markets and friendly people were part of the city, poverty, and insecurity were a constant reminder that not everyone could benefit from the city's blessings.

I could never forget this feeling of helplessness. I knew I had been fortunate to grow up in such a wonderful place, with so many resources that one could benefit from if they decided to work on their creativity in my city. As a little girl, I said to myself, "One day, I am going to make sure all my dreams come true," knowing I have a bright future ahead of me. I was a little girl with a sense of understanding of what was happening, but deep inside, despite my little heart, I knew there was more out there for me.

For me, the city was an unequaled source of love and beauty, and I was eager and determined to give back and share that love with the people I cared about. I was determined to make a difference in the lives of those who weren't as lucky as me. It was my way to honor the city that had been my home for the past half of my childhood. Unfortunately, it never happened. All I could do was to bear the love for them inside my heart and pray to God to bless them both with good health and financially.

As a little girl, I preferred to play alone instead of joining with other children every afternoon or evening. I always end up being encouraged by others to go and play with my fellow kids, but I couldn't seem to find the connection I was looking for.

At times, I would try to be involved; however, I would often end up alone again. But I was content with my own time. So, I will always spend hours playing in the dirty sand and exploring my small world, leaving the other children to have fun together.

My mother was worried about my preference for solitude, but I also knew that I was a strong and independent girl. My mother could tell that I was different, and she respected that.

Growing up, I began to know why I always stayed in my own company. I was an introvert who found energy and comfort in my own company.

I learned to embrace my introverted nature and the peace it brought me. I found a sense of belonging in my own thoughts and inner world. I was content to enjoy my own company and no longer felt the need to try and fit in with those around me.

My mother was relieved to see me happy and content with my company. She knew my introversion was a part of my personality, and she accepted it with love and understanding.

***

Growing up, I experienced a considerable amount of spiritual warfare throughout my childhood. Many aspects of my life left me wondering how certain events were intertwined, but one thing was clear - these interventions could only be explained as God's work.

From my earliest memories, I recall finding myself in unexpected situations that seemed impossible to escape. Yet, time and time again, I managed to come out unscathed. It was like an invisible hand guided me, protecting me from harm and leading me to safety.

I faced numerous health challenges as a young child. I fell ill frequently, and my fragile body seemed incapable of fighting off even the mildest of infections. However, by the grace of God, I mustered the strength to persevere. I cannot explain the inner resilience that kept me going, but it was undoubtedly a gift from above.

Throughout my journey, I sought solace in my unwavering faith. I found comfort in knowing that even during the darkest and most challenging times, I believed God was beside me along the way. The battles I faced were not merely physical or emotional as they were spiritual. Yet, I knew that with God's intervention, I would triumph.

As I continued to reflect on my childhood, I am grateful for the divine protection I experienced. Each hurdle I overcame is a testament to God's love and guidance. My struggles may not always have had clear explanations, but my unwavering faith in the almighty power of God carried me through. Looking back on those formative years, I realize these trials shaped my character and strengthened my resolve. They taught me the value of perseverance, trust, and resilience, and qualities that continue to influence my life today.

As a little girl not knowing who God was, I only understood Him from my parents' teaching about Biblical stories and how He saved His people. I applied that knowledge by acknowledging the miracles and divine interventions that shaped my life. I am forever indebted to God's grace, and without it, I would not be standing here today.

Looking back on my childhood, I was reminiscent of a spiritual battlefield filled with mysteries and inexplicable events. But through it all, God's intervention shone brightly, safeguarding me and providing me with the strength to overcome adversity. Today, I stand as a grateful witness to a mighty God who guided me through the trials of childhood and continues to illuminate my path.

Growing up, I experienced a considerable amount of spiritual warfare throughout my childhood. Many aspects of my life left me wondering how certain events were intertwined, but one thing was clear - these interventions could only be explained as God's work. From my earliest memories, I recall finding myself in unexpected situations that seemed impossible to escape. Yet, time and time again, I managed to come out unscathed. It was like an invisible hand guided me, protecting me from harm and leading me to safety.

***

And throughout my childhood days. I had a deep passion for music that resided within my very soul. Whenever my mother or sisters and I would pass by the church on our way home in the evenings, we would often hear the beautiful melodies of the choir practicing. Each note and lyric resonated with me and filled my heart with a profound sense of peace and joy.

During those moments, there was something inexplicable that stirred within me. As a young child, I lacked the understanding to articulate my emotions. I was unaware of the profound spiritual connection being forged within me, as I had yet to comprehend the concept of God.

As time went on, my love for music only grew stronger. I found solace in the gentle harmonies and uplifting rhythms. Music became my refuge, a place where I could escape the complexities of this world and immerse myself in the beauty of sound.

In a still little age of my childhood, my curiosity for music intensified. I sought every opportunity to learn more about different instruments, styles, and genres. I would attend church with my family every Sabbath day during the weekend on the 7th day of the week, participate in church activities such as adventure club, and listen to countless albums purchased from my parents. Music became a constant companion, guiding me through the ups and downs of life.

My love for music began to grow deeper into spiritual songs. My curiosity was to learn more about the historical events that occurred in making my music and what made the people write those songs. I had no answer to that question. I started to feel the emotions from the inside of my heart and how my heart shifted as I listened to the songs or heard them. Looking back, I could sense that music can heal, unite, and inspire. I came to recognize that the emotions I had experienced as a child, listening to the choir in the church, were a manifestation of a spiritual connection to something greater than myself.

The realization struck me one day when I witnessed a powerful performance at church. The choir on stage possessed a genuine passion that radiated through their music, connecting with the souls of everyone in the audience. At that moment, I felt an overwhelming joy and peace within my heart. I could also sense something more within me that I couldn't explain or put into words. As a little child, I didn't know who God was. I remember my parents teaching me and my siblings to pray wherever we are. I would always speak to God everywhere I go and every place I am.

***

I remember the day we left the Shinyanga Region. We had small belongings with us as we traveled while the rest of our belongings shipped. I am trying to remember how my parents transported the rest of my belongings. With all our belongings coming with us on the long journey, everything was coming. Nothing could contain anything that could replace all the things we had to leave behind.

My dad got promoted to a job opportunity as an accountant, and he had to take it. So, we had to leave our hometown, friends, and the places we had grown up around.

AMID MY QUESTIONABLE EXISTENCE

The first couple of days were hard. Everything was new. All the sounds, smells, and atmosphere were completely different from what we used to. But things began to settle when we started making friends and exploring all the opportunities that were finally available.

That great moment was the best thing that ever occurred to my family. We could never have achieved what we achieved if not for the courage of my father and the determination and adventurous spirit of my mother.

Fast-forward to today, and I can see the bigger picture. I can see how all the struggles, all the things we had to leave behind, and all the new opportunities available to us had made us strong, and I realize the importance of family, hard work, and patience.

My family and I have traveled far and experienced amazing things. But in the end, the move to Dar-es-Salaam brought us closer together and taught us how to appreciate life's wonders.

When I first moved to Dar-es-Salaam, I expected a significant change from the small town I had left behind. The bustling city seemed practically like a different world, but I found it hard to connect with the locals despite my attempts to fit in.

After moving to a new city, we reached the neighborhood called Mwemberadu, located in Kigamboni, where we first arrived on our journey. That is the place where my family and I reside. A few months passed, and my parents decided it was time for my sisters and I to start school. Excited and a little nervous all at once. I was eager to begin our new school year. We had the bonus of being able to go to school together, as my sisters and I were starting school in different grades. Me and my little sister and I ended up studying a few blocks away from home compared to my big sister, Happiness.

Living at Mwemberadu as a little girl, I had the privilege of continuing my education at Consolata Nursery School alongside my little sister. The school was a haven of tranquility, surrounded by the beauty of nature. The gentle breeze carried the scent of fresh air, and the shade provided by the trees offered respite during the scorching afternoons.

The children at Consolata Nursery School were a delight to be around. We formed lasting friendships and embraced each other's company. The camaraderie that blossomed between us made our days at school joyful and memorable.

One aspect of my personality that stayed with me during those early years was my habit of humming songs. It became my second nature when I played with my classmates and sometimes as we engaged in our activities. I spontaneously create melodies and lyrics, weaving together a random song. I entertained my friends and added an extra layer of creativity and excitement to our playtime.

The teachers at Consolata Nursery School played a pivotal role in our development. They were not only knowledgeable and dedicated, but they also had a genuine passion for nurturing young minds. Their professional approach to education instilled in us a deep love for learning and exploration. They encouraged us to think critically, ask questions, and express our ideas freely. With their guidance, we developed a solid foundation for academic success.

I reflected on my time at Consolata Nursery School. I am grateful for the beautiful experiences and opportunities it provided. The school's serene environment, coupled with the genuine camaraderie among the students and the guidance of the exceptional teachers, shaped me into the person I am today. It instilled in me a love for nature, a passion for music, and a thirst for knowledge that continues to drive me forward.

Consolata Nursery School holds a special place in my heart, as it not only fostered my early academic growth but also nurtured my character and instilled values that have guided me throughout my life. The memories created in those formative years shall forever remain etched in my mind as a constant reminder of the transformative power of education and the impact of knowledge it filled in my life.

My time at Consolata Nursery School was a cherished chapter in my life. It laid the foundation for my future endeavors and ignited a lifelong pursuit of knowledge and self-discovery. I will forever be grateful for the beautiful experiences, friendships, and lessons I gained at this remarkable institution.

My little sister and I later transitioned from one school to another at Kigamboni. Kigamboni District, officially known as the

AMID MY QUESTIONABLE EXISTENCE

Kigamboni Municipal Council, is one of the five districts of the Dar es Salaam Region of Tanzania. It is known for its beautiful beaches and the number of tourists.

I went to study first grade at Kigamboni Primary School. I remember the school campus was big, surrounded by trees with different-colored bricks in the walls, with many playgrounds inside the school surrounded by a long and tall fence. And the beauty of green colors surrounded the school.

After a year of moving to a new city with my family staying at Mwemberadu, I noticed everyone seemed too wrapped up in their lives to bother with anybody, and the culture shock was something I was surprised by. I spent my days quietly observing the people of Dar-es-Salaam, trying to understand why I felt so alone despite being in a densely populated area. I was determined to learn to acclimate to my new surroundings, even if my efforts had yet to progress.

One day, I stumbled across an area that seemed filled with people from all walks of life. I was eager to learn more about the practice and the various cultures of the people within the class. Despite my worries about standing out, I found that the sense of calm and mutual acceptance within the group would help me relax. It was the first time I felt like I belonged and welcomed by my new community. However, deep inside me, it was different. It's not that I didn't belong in a circle with the people around me. There are moments when I wouldn't fit in because that group, person, place, or relationship was not for me.

After a short period, the class quickly became part of my weekly routine, meeting new people. I finally shed my sense of separation, learning to adapt to the area and start a life in Dar-es-Salaam that felt more like home.

Despite this being a big transition, I kept my composure and found it hard to connect with others and fit in. Most of the time, I think of what I should do and what my future will be. And who I want to become. It kept running into my mind. Still, music was one of my favorite things as a little girl. I always found a way to soothe myself through music, making some random lyrics and recalling the songs I've listened to at home.

Growing up in the city of Dar-es-Salaam was a fascinating experience. As a child, I exposed myself to different lessons each year. I learned how to read the Bible when nobody was looking. I also learned the value of hard work and patience. I was able to witness my village slowly transformed over the years.

With the introduction of technology and economic changes, the big city of Dar-es-Salaam quickly became a vibrant neighborhood. Each year, more and more people moved in, bringing in new ideas and ways of life.

As I continued to grow, I began to recognize the importance of understanding history and looking forward to the future. I noticed how the city had started to embrace the changes and how it had become an integral part of the larger world around it. At this point, I began to appreciate the power of community and the importance of looking out for each other.

On other days, I became more aware of the world beyond my big city. I yearned to see different places, encounter new people, and experience life outside my comfort zone.

On every other day, I would find a way to explore new places. I never worried about the language barrier or any social boundaries. I followed my curiosity everywhere it led me. Though I enjoyed my time away from home, I always kept sight of what mattered most at home.

On the weekends, especially Sundays, I spent time with my family, especially my little sister. I would play with her in our backyard, go to the park, or watch cartoons on the couch. As a reminder of home and the familiarity I always felt even when I was far away.

At the end of each weekend, I found solace in how I had spent my two days. I had gone out to experience the world, learning new things. But I had also returned home to spend time with those I loved most. My two worlds found a balance, allowing me to expand my horizons and stay grounded in the true importance of life.

***

After a few years of staying at Mwemberadu, we finally moved into the new neighborhood, 10 minutes from Kigamboni SDA Church. I was surprised by how nice it was. Everybody was friendly and welcoming, and there were plenty of places to explore. After my parents bought a house a few distance from church, the area had plenty of activities for me to do in my free time.

I quickly made friends with some of the local kids including Rose, Kibibi, Felista, Otto, Paul, Frida, Witi, Monica, Eudia, Maua, Penina, Francis, Joram, Vicent, Nelly, Jennifer, Janneth, Abdul, and other kids. I also began to take some classes at church. The people from the church were so kind and generous, teaching me about faith and helping me grow in spirit. I even joined the youth group, which opened a new world of friends and opportunities.

It felt like home almost immediately, and I soon settled into a new routine with my new family and friends. On weekdays to weekends, we would all meet up after school to grab some ice cream and play rede (a sport where two teams come together and people from the other team throw the ball and one person or four people standing in the middle to catch the ball and whoever get hit by the ball is out until the last person remaining to win on behalf of their team) outside our houses, and enjoy each other's company. It's hard to believe it's already been two years since we moved in. It may have started as a fresh start, but it's grown into so much more.

I remember meeting one of the young children at church, including Monica and Eudia, who became my long-term best friends and sisters at heart. We were a diverse group with different personalities and backgrounds and formed a strong bond that lasted through the years.

Among my friends, Francis was a quiet and introverted young boy. While he may not have been the loudest voice in the group, his wisdom and thoughtfulness always left a lasting impact on us. For some reason, through Francis, I learned the importance of focus and reflection and how sometimes the most profound moments are found in stillness.

Joram, on the other hand, had a wild and funny personality. He was always the life of the party, cracking jokes and making us laugh until our stomachs hurt. Joram taught me the power of laughter and how it can bring joy and lightness to even the darkest situations.

Together, we joined the Adventure Club founded by the Seventh Day Adventists Church, a group that embarked on countless escapades and explored the world with childlike wonder. Our adventures took us to mountain peaks, deep forests, and unknown territories. In those moments of exploration, we discovered the beauty and vastness of the world, and it fueled our curiosity and thirst for knowledge.

But what made our club truly special was our former teacher. She was a wise and compassionate soul who saw the potential in each of us. Our teacher guided us with her gentleness and words of encouragement and imparted her wisdom to us. She taught us the value of perseverance, kindness, and embracing our uniqueness.

Unfortunately, our precious teacher passed away, leaving a void in our hearts. However, her teachings and the memories we shared with her lived on within us. Her encouragement and wisdom became a guiding light, shaping our lives even after she was gone.

Years went by, and we grew up. Monica, Eudia, Francis, Joram, and the rest of the group members continued to pursue different paths in life, but our bond remained unbreakable. Through joys and sorrows, triumphs and failures, we remain a support system for one another. Our teacher guided us with gentle words of encouragement and imparted her wisdom. She taught us the value of perseverance, kindness, and embracing our uniqueness.

Within the club, I was viewed by others as a quiet one. As part of my personality, I was analytical and focused. I was known for my problem-solving skills while working hard to be on top of everything. Most of the time, I would receive the task of leading the group a few times.

I also was the shy one who was kind and gentle. Everybody knew me to be the listener, not because I had no idea what to say, but because I wanted to understand and consider every part of the conversation. I loved to help others out, and my encouraging nature made me approachable.

Looking back, I realize how fortunate I was to have crossed paths with these incredible individuals. The Adventure Club not only taught me about the world and its wonders but also about the power of friendship and the lasting impact we can have on one another.

As I continue my journey, I carry with me the memories of our adventures, the lessons taught by our teacher, and the love shared by

Monica, Eudia, Francis, Joram, and the entire Adventure Club members. Their presence in my life has shaped me into the person I am today, and for that, I am eternally grateful.

A year later, I went to study at another school outside of Kigamboni. On the first day of school, we all hopped in the car, me, my sister, and our parents—we both went on our daily activities. My dad went to work, and my sister and mother went to school. The school I studied in was around a 10 to 20-minute walk from the office where my dad used to work. The school building was tall, filled with different-colored bricks in the walls, and the playgrounds differed from the ones we had back home. It felt strange to be standing at the new school's entrance, and I couldn't help the little knot of nerves in my stomach.

But my worries and fears were soon pushed aside, as I followed my mom as she was also a teacher at the school we transferred "Bunge Primary School" with my little sister to the office where we would find out about our classes. My mom had all the paperwork filled out the year before we started, and we soon found out our schedules. My sister and I got different homeroom teachers as we were in different grades, so that made me feel a little nervous. I wished we'd at least have one class where we were together.

Before long, it was time for us to go to our classes. We said goodbye to our mother, and she hugged us while saying we had to have fun learning and watched us go. I took my littlest sister's hand in mine. I could tell she was just as nervous as I was, so I squeezed her hand tightly, trying to give her courage on the way to class.

We made our separate ways to our homerooms. Soon, I went to my homeroom class, located at the end of the hallway corner. The teacher introduced me to other kids in the class, who welcomed me both with warm smiles. And with that, I knew that even though I was in a new school, I would be okay.

My little sister, Mbuke, and I have always been learners. Before school, we would excitedly go through hour-long lectures and read books available at our sweetest home. In kindergarten, our parents will decide to send us to small private schools close to our home. We loved our teachers and learned many new things about the world. Despite moving around a lot, It had been hard to adjust as we moved cross-country, away from our old neighbors and all the memories we had made there. But when my parents decided to move closer to the church, I was happy to go along with it, and it was a fresh start in a new place, a chance to build new relationships and make new memories.

***

For part of my childhood, I had the habit of praying and talking to God every single time of day while walking or doing any activity. It has been a custom that I found myself doing since I was a little child before and after starting to go to school. I may not even know or have the knowledge of God in my life as a little child. Still deep inside my heart, through my conscious mind, I could feel the comfort and peace inside my heart in the presence of God and through the music I listened to.

I remember it was a beautiful Friday afternoon, the sun casting its warm glow upon the bustling streets of my small town. School had just ended, and the joyful anticipation of the weekend had filled the air.

Bunge Primary School was always a place of learning and love, where children were taught academic knowledge and valuable life lessons. Road safety was one such lesson instilled in us from a young age. We were introduced to always look left and right before crossing the road, ensuring our safety and well-being.

I cautiously approached the busy intersection near the ferry station with this knowledge. The sound of car horns and chatter filled the air as people hurriedly made their way across the road. Standing at the crosswalk, I surveyed the route, meticulously checking for any approaching vehicles.

Feeling confident it was safe to proceed, I bravely took my first step onto the white zebra crossing. But fate had something else in store for me that day. In that split second, as if time had slowed to a crawl, a Daladala, the local bus, appeared out of nowhere, hurtling towards me with alarming speed.

Fear gripped my heart as I instinctively covered my face with my trembling right hand. I braced myself, expecting the worst. It felt like an eternity had passed before the Daladala collided with me. The impact sent shockwaves through my body, but miraculously, I felt no pain. It was like I was encased in a protective shield of divine intervention.

Through the haze of disbelief, I could hear the panicked cries and screams of those around me. Amongst the chaos, a woman standing nearby, engrossed in conversation on her phone, reacted swiftly. With lightning speed and strength I hadn't expected, she reached out and grabbed my trembling body.

She pulled me away from the road to safety with care and urgency. Tears welled in her eyes as she assessed the scene and realized the magnitude of what had just happened. The bus driver, visibly shaken, parked the Daladala to the side and rushed over to check on me, a tremor of concern in his voice.

"Are you okay, little girl?" he asked, his eyes filled with genuine worry. Despite the shock, I managed to summon a calm voice and replied, "Yes, sir, I am perfectly fine. Don't worry." The woman beside me hugged me tightly, her gratitude and relief evident in her embrace.

As I continued my journey to the ferry, one thought consumed my mind: gratitude. Gratitude for my safety, for the miraculous protection that had shielded me from harm. I couldn't help but cry tears of mixed emotions, overwhelmed by the realization that I had been given a second chance at life.

At that moment, walking towards the water's edge, I whispered a heartfelt thank you to the heavens above. My heart overflowed with a profound sense of awe, and I wondered about the supernatural miracle I had just experienced. It reminded us that something greater than us is watching over us in times of peril.

Since that fateful day, I have carried the memory of that incident with me as a constant reminder of the fragility of life and the power of faith. It is a testament to the undeniable force of miracles, an invisible hand guiding and protecting us even in dire circumstances.

So, as I stepped onto the ferry, surrounded by the myriad of bustling individuals,

I felt an overwhelming sense of purpose. In the deepest recesses of my soul, I knew that I had been spared for a reason. With every beat of my grateful heart, I vowed to live each moment to its fullest, cherishing the gift of life and the supernatural miracles that grace us in the blink of an eye.

The following year, our parents moved us to a different school. We'd go from public to private schools and back, searching for the one that offered the best teaching. Every school had a different perspective, curriculum, and expectations for us. Still, no matter where we went, Mbuke and I were always in the same school or different school locations and then joined each other together.

This continued until we reached middle school. We finally settled on a prestigious public school only for a few years that offered a comprehensive and challenging curriculum and was close enough for our family to stay for several years. Great teachers encouraged us to take risks and learn as much as possible.

In middle school, my sister and I had been studying at Bunge Primary School for two years when our parents decided to move us to a different school. Although I was sad to leave my old friends, I was excited to start a new adventure. The lowest part of this, I didn't have a great time studying at that school.

One day, I came to school with Underwear inside my bag. I didn't know that there was underwear inside my bag. The underwear was more significant compared to my size as a little girl. I didn't quite remember how it entered; I usually habitually checked on my school bag in my room before going to school. That was the worst day of my life. When I say the worst, I mean the worst; one of my classmates asked for something to borrow from me. She entered the bag, saw this vast underwear, and lifted it to the whole class as they laughed. I felt embarrassed and humiliated. There were also times when I ended up being accused of something which I didn't do by other students. I had to go on with my day. I said to myself, will I ever forget this embarrassing moment in my life?

As a student, I've always learned or processed things at the lowest phase; everything went slowly. I've always wanted to catch up with other students. However, for the most part, it always has the same results. I can also say it was only by God's grace that I could finish my yearly courses.

***

In the serene neighborhood of Kigamboni, my family and I had the pleasure of forming an extraordinary bond with the esteemed Kipilyango family. Mr. and Mrs. Kipilyango quickly became our second grandparents, as their warm embrace and kind hearts repeatedly beckoned us to their humble abode. Their residence, conveniently situated not too far away from our own, allowed for regular visits that brought about countless cherished memories.

In the heart of this close-knit community, we carved out a haven of love and friendship.

Every moment spent at the Kipilyangos, they embraced us in a wave of joy and tranquility. As if touched by divine fate, our connection blossomed effortlessly, weaving the fabric of our lives together.

Our house was a mere ten-minute stroll away from the local church, where we devoutly congregated every week. This proximity allowed us to attend church services punctually and conveniently placed us within reach of the Kipilyangos' dwelling. It was as if destiny had lovingly entwined our lives, ensuring each encounter was effortlessly woven into our routines.

On Sundays or during weekday afternoons, my parents would organize a visit to our beloved second grandparents. They understood the profound bond I had developed with the Kipilyango family, and seeing their genuine smiles each time my excitement grew only deepened their affection for our dear friends.

As we embarked on these cherished journeys to Mr. and Mrs. Kipilyango's dwelling, anticipation nestled within our hearts. The picturesque surroundings captivated us at every turn, with the vibrant greenery and colorful flora breathing life into the landscape. Birds sang melodious tunes, seemingly rejoicing in the love that flowed freely in this haven of familiarity.

Arriving at the floral gate that guarded the Kipilyango residence, we were greeted by the harmonious combination of laughter and delightful chatter that echoed through the air. The rustling of leaves whispered enchanting tales of unity and camaraderie.

Mrs. Kipilyango, with her warm and enchanting smile, enveloped us in the comforting aroma of freshly baked cookies. Crafted with love, these culinary delights delighted our taste buds, confirming that the moments shared with this family were magical.

Meanwhile, Mr. Kipilyango emanated wisdom and experience, his stories captivating young and old alike. Through his animated gestures and lively voice, he breathed life into tales of adventures long past, captivating our imaginations and eliciting unabashed laughter.

Within this harmonious haven, they seemed to dance at their own pace. Days turned into weeks, which then effortlessly transformed into months, but our bond remained unwavering. The Kipilyango family had become an indispensable part of our lives, reflecting love and kinship in its purest form.

As I look back years after those cherished moments, my heart swells with gratitude for our deep connection with the Kipilyangos. Our proximity to one another allowed for frequent visits, creating an unbreakable bond between families and generations. The love we shared within those walls transcended any distance or time.

And the memories created at Kigamboni will forever be etched in the fabric of our lives. The love extended by the Kipilyango family, their kitchen filled with mouthwatering aromas, and their hearts overflowing with warmth will forever remain a testament to the power of friendship and family.

***

In the beautiful coastal city of Kigamboni, I engaged in countless adventures alongside my cherished little sister. We were two peas in a pod, inseparable in our quest for merriment and mischief. Amidst our spirited escapades, one place held a special place in our hearts – the humble abode of Sister Nkwaya, the esteemed wife of a renowned pastor, Singo.

The resonating laughter of children often reverberated through the air as we embarked on our daily pilgrimage to this delightful haven. Our tiny feet would step lightly on the cobbled path, excited to meet Sister Nkwaya's precious treasure – the adorable baby Santi. Although Santi hadn't mastered crawling or sitting, her enchanting presence enthralled us.

Sister Nkwaya welcomed us into their warm sanctuary every morning with open arms. The familiar scent of freshly brewed morning tea mingled with the soft lullabies that emanated from the baby's nursery. We would embark on a playful journey of imaginative play, where reality danced harmoniously with make-believe.

From painting colorful landscapes on blank canvases to constructing wondrous castles with toy blocks, the world became a canvas for our youthful creativity. Endless stories would unravel as we stitched together vivid tapestries of imagination, effortlessly transcending the confines of time and space.

As the sun traversed its astronomical path, casting gentle rays of warmth upon our playful souls, the hours seemed to melt away like caramel under the scorching equatorial sun. Sister Nkwaya would join our happy company from time to time, enchanting us with her gentle wisdom and tender warmth.

In this serene haven, it was not just playtime that nourished our spirits but also the profound bond we developed with Santi. Though she may not have been able to join us in our daring adventure, her innocent laughter and cherubic smile bound us together in an unbreakable embrace of love.

Every visit to Sister Nkwaya's house was preceded by a courteous phone call, ensuring our presence would not disturb their daily routine. It was a testament to our mutual respect for one another's lives. This simple gesture infused our adventures with an air of anticipation and reinforced the bond between our families.

As the moon began its ascent into the vast tapestry of night, signaling the time to bid farewell, we would reluctantly say our goodbyes to Sister Nkwaya and her family. Our hearts were heavy with a blend of contentment and longing, yearning for the following day when we would return to this place again.

Time moved incessantly, as it always does, carrying us away from our beloved Kigamboni and onto new horizons. Yet, even now, the memory of those joyous days spent with Sister Nkwaya, playing with little Santi, fills my heart with warmth. It reminds me of the sanctity of those childhood moments, unburdened by the weight of responsibility and the world's demands.

The legacy of Sister Nkwaya's gentle spirit lives on, encapsulated in the ethereal memories we shared within the walls of her home. Regardless of time, the bond we formed and the unconditional love we discovered in that humble home will forever be etched upon our lives' tapestry.

So, dear reader, I implore you to venture into Sister Nkwaya's haven if you seek solace or respite. There, you may find echoes of our laughter, imprints of our painted hands, and perhaps even glimpse little Santi as she begins her extraordinary journey.

***

The following year, my little sister and I enrolled at Diamond International Primary School, a much bigger school than Bunge. We were lucky enough to be able to pick up our studies and continue moving forward with our grades. The teachers were friendly and welcoming, and we quickly settled into our new routine.

> Great teachers encouraged us to take risks and learn as much as possible.

My sister and I quickly made some new friends at Diamond International Primary School, and it was soon that we were having lots of fun in our classes and during recess. We shared stories of our old school and made lots of exciting discoveries about our new one. One thing about us is that we were both very different in character and personality. There were times when my sister's friends, who were also my friends, some of them including Queen, Sethi, and Amy, used to say, "Mbuke, your sister is so quiet!" I would stand there and say nothing but smile at them. We first met at the waiting stop for our school bus at our former school, Bunge Primary School.

While studying at Diamond International Primary School, my friends Queen, Sethi, Amy, my little sister, and I would meet each other every morning outside the gate of Bunge Primary School, eagerly waiting for the school bus to arrive. This was our daily routine, and we stuck together from morning till afternoon after school, and even during the time we would leave for school. We had formed an unbreakable bond.

We had a special place, a little corner of our own, where we would gather before heading to the bus station to go home. It was a small courtyard surrounded by trees, providing tranquility amidst the bustling school environment. This place was significant for us as it became a sanctuary where we shared our joys, sorrows, and dreams.

Every morning, the five of us would arrive at the same time, often laughing and joking as we greeted each other. Always confident, Queen would lead the way, her smile brightening the courtyard. With her gentle demeanor, Sethi was the silent observer, ready to lend a listening ear whenever we needed one. Amy, a friend, had an infectious energy that was contagious. And my little sister, always a bundle of joy, brought laughter and innocence to our group.

As we sat in our particular spot, time seemed to move differently. We would talk about everything under the sun, from school assignments to our dreams for the future. We shared our fears and aspirations, giving each other the strength to overcome hurdles and chase our goals. Together, we were a support system, uplifting and motivating one another.

The memories we created in that particular place are etched in my heart. It was a place where we celebrated birthdays, shared secrets, and shed tears during tough times. We formed a bond that extended beyond the confines of the courtyard. We became a family, always there for each other through thick and thin.

Whether it was summer's scorching heat or winter's chilly winds, we never missed our daily meeting at that spot. Rain or shine, we would huddle under the shelter of the trees, finding solace in each other's presence. Those moments fortified our friendship, and I am grateful for every minute we spent there.

As time passed, we departed to a different path after studying at Diamond International Primary School. We went to look at another school, but the memories of that particular place and our bond remained intact. Although distance may have separated us physically, our friendship endured, and we grew individually while always being connected at heart.

Looking back, I realize that those moments at the particular place were the most cherished of my primary school years. The laughter, the tears, and everything in between shaped who I am today. The lessons I learned from my friends during those treasured moments continue to guide me.

The bond my friends and I formed at our special place outside Bunge Primary School holds a special place in my story. It exemplifies the power of friendship and the ability of a familiar spot to become a beacon of love, support, and shared experiences. No matter where life takes us, those moments will forever remain a treasure I will never forget.

***

AMID MY QUESTIONABLE EXISTENCE

Though we had only been at Diamond International briefly, we already felt like it had become our new home. We spent much of our free time exploring every corner of the school, playing outdoor games with our classmates, and attending the afternoon activities.

I was grateful that our family had chosen Diamond International Primary School, and I know my sister felt the same way. After just one year, I felt like I'd been attending the school much longer. I was firmly entrenched in the school's culture and looking forward to another adventurous year here.

After a few years of studying at Diamond International Primary School, I went to join my little sister to learn 6th grade at another private school called Fray Luis Amigo Primary School before transferring to Mahenge Pre & Primary School English Medium to finish my final grade level where we both ended up studying together again years later, and that was the school where I would be spending my last year of studying primary school before I moved on to the next chapter of my life from being a primary schooler to a secondary student.

Studying at Fray Luis Amigo Primary School was one of the most unique moments in my life. It provided a comforting environment where I could pursue my education alongside familiar faces from my church community. Among the familiar faces were Francis, Joram, Neema, and Mr. Mika, my neighbors Francisca and the Miringa siblings.

AMID MY QUESTIONABLE EXISTENCE

Set amidst lush green surroundings, the school boasted a natural landscape filled with vibrant grass and trees. Fray Luis Amigo Primary School was distinctive in its division into three sections catering to students at different levels: Kindergarten, Primary, and Secondary.

This serene and nature-filled ambiance significantly contributed to my overall learning experience. The tranquil environment allowed me to focus on my studies and develop a solid academic foundation. The school's proximity to my home and the presence of familiar faces further enhanced my comfort level, making learning a joyful endeavor.

At Fray Luis Amigo Primary School, I had the opportunity to acquire knowledge and build lasting friendships. The companionship of

Francis, Joram, Neema, and the Miringa siblings made everyday school life more enjoyable and fostered collaboration in our academic pursuits. Together, we faced educational challenges, celebrated achievements, and grew as individuals.

I must also acknowledge the dedication and guidance the school's teachers provided, particularly Mr. Mika, who served as a respected educator and a familiar figure from our church community. His teaching methods and expertise helped shape his academic growth, while his support and encouragement motivated us to reach the students' full potential.

At the same time, it was hard to focus on school as I was in the middle of academic adversity. Not only at Fray Louis Amigo, among the schools I've studied before, I kept experiencing the same situation, hoping I would be like other students.

As I reminisce about my time at Fray Luis Amigo Primary School, I realize how fortunate I was to be part of such a nurturing educational institution. Combining natural surroundings, familiar faces, and dedicated teachers created an enriching and empowering learning environment. It laid the foundation for my personal and academic growth, instilling in me a love for learning and a sense of belonging that has stayed with me.

My experience at Fray Luis Amigo Primary School holds a special place in my heart. It was a time of cherished memories, lasting friendships, and transformative learning. Grateful for the opportunities and support I received, I carry the lessons learned and the connections forged during those years throughout my life's journey.

In 2011, which marked the conclusion of my 7th grade at Mahenge Pre & Primary School English Medium and all my primary school years. I was fortunate to be blessed with exceptional teachers who imparted knowledge and instilled in us a sense of inspiration and encouragement. Though the school boasted a modest number of students, it provided a warm and friendly atmosphere that fostered a memorable educational experience.

Throughout my time at Mahenge School, I encountered numerous challenges in understanding certain subjects. However, my determination fueled my efforts to work diligently and strive for excellence. With the grace of God, I persevered and excelled in all my classes until my final year of graduation.

Reflecting upon those formative years, I am genuinely grateful for the valuable opportunities bestowed upon me. The wonderful and caring teachers at Mahenge School imparted knowledge and served as role models, nurturing a sense of responsibility, discipline, and ambition within me.

As I bid farewell to my final year of primary school 7th grade and prepare to embark on new educational adventures, I carry the memories and lessons learned at Mahenge Pre & Primary School English Medium. The guidance and support I received from my teachers have left an indelible mark on my academic journey, shaping me into the individual I am today.

With a heart full of gratitude, I anticipate the challenges and triumphs that lie ahead, knowing that the foundation laid by Mahenge School and the past schools I attended has equipped me with the skills and determination necessary to navigate the path to success.

I remember, growing up, my sister and I were the two halves of the same coin. Everywhere we go, people would comment on our different personalities and characters. While she was outgoing and the life of so many activities around her, I was more reserved and introverted. We went to the same school for all our elementary and middle grades. No matter which school we both attended, we'll be told about our different personalities and characters. The only word that I heard often was "Your sister is so quiet?" or "Why is your sister so quiet?" and "You guys look so much different from each other?". There are moments in my class where one of the students would toss out, "She looks different," or "She's different from everyone else," which would immediately draw scowls from the teachers.

Despite the comments, my sister and I were close. I had my friends and was comfortable being the reserved girl in the corner while she spent her time with the more loud and outgoing types. As different as we were, we never let it separate us. We were more alike than we were different. Differences in personalities don't make a family love. That was a lesson my sister and I learned growing up, and it made us closer as siblings and friends.

***

When I was growing up in Dar-es-Salaam, I felt like I was escaping the monotony of my small-town life. I fell deeper into the vibrancy and daily activities of the city and the culture that surrounded me. There was so much to learn, and I was passionate about understanding the people, the customs, the language, and the food. I was eager to explore the world around me and embrace every new opportunity that came my way.

I look back fondly on the years I spent growing up in Dar-es-Salaam. I got exposed to something truly unique. It shaped the way I think and helped me to gain a better understanding of my place in the world. I learned how to navigate the city and interacted with locals and travelers. Life in the city had a lot of different backgrounds and cultures, and this experience enabled me to be more understanding and knowledgeable of the world.

Despite the chaos and hustle of the city, there was a sense of calm and tranquility. I would spend hours exploring the local markets, scooping up new spices and foods, and immersing myself in the city. The past and present are mixed, creating a truly unique and inspirational atmosphere. I began to understand that the past and present are equally significant to keeping our culture alive and that we must appreciate and learn from our past to inform our future.

AMID MY QUESTIONABLE EXISTENCE

Looking back on my time in Dar-es-Salaam, I am thankful for the lessons that taught me. It has helped me to understand that looking forward to the future is just as important as examining and understanding the past. This lesson has allowed me to be open to new ideas and other cultures and either challenge my beliefs or accept them with respect and appreciation. Dar-es-Salaam is a city of vibrancy and diversity. I will always remember the lessons it taught me and the experiences I had growing up, that the past and present are equally significant to keep our culture alive and that we must appreciate and learn from our past to inform our future.

CHAPTER 2

ONE STEP AT A TIME: WORKING TO UNDERSTAND A CLEAR BIG PICTURE OF WHAT TO DO NEXT

As a child growing up in the bustling city of Dar-es-Salaam, I was inspired by the rich culture surrounding me. Music was everywhere – in the bustling marketplace, the car horns blaring in the streets, and the beautiful voices of the Tanzanian people that filled the air. Everywhere I looked, I saw music and was captivated by it.

From a young age, I felt a profound connection to music. In school, I practiced singing while my classmates murmured and looked at me curiously. I didn't understand why I felt so connected to it, but all I knew was that I needed to make music my life's work.

After school, I would pursue making minor music with every ounce of my being, singing all along, and trying different styles from contemporary songs. I soon began to immerse myself in the rich Tanzanian music scene, attending live performances and studying different types of music. I was particularly drawn to the traditional folk music of my homeland and soon found myself putting my unique spin on it, combining classic styles with more contemporary sounds.

Throughout my childhood life, compared to most of my peers. I was always known as the quiet one in my group of friends. It was like I had a switch that I could turn off. I was never the loudest or most outgoing kid. I was content to observe and take in the scenery.

My parents always encouraged me to be outgoing and speak up more often, but it never worked. I was just comfortable being the quiet kid.

My friends and family knew I was always there, but I wouldn't participate in conversations or activities unless asked to. I was the one who sat back and watched how others interacted, taking mental notes of the dynamics between people.

I remember some of my friends were continually baffled by my ability to sit back and observe. They'd ask why I was so quiet, and I'd smile and say, "That's just me."

In hindsight, I'm grateful for who I was and for being the quiet one in my group. I could take in the moments and remember them for what they were. I felt I could better view the world by being quiet and observing.

My childhood was full of moments of quiet observation, and I wouldn't trade those moments for the world.

At 9, as an ordinary young girl living in Dar-es-Salaam, I had one goal: to become a singer and inspire the world through my music. While many of my peers had already devised plans and dreams for their future, I continued exploring my aspirations more.

Every Sunday and Saturday morning, I was up an hour before dawn after praying a short prayer thanking God for waking me up. While still in bed, I recall the songs I made up and the lyrics of the songs I've written in my head. I would always write down the poems I've come up with in the small notebook or paper as a final touch, just in case I forget.

When I finally have a full version of the song I wrote, I will spend time and time practicing and memorizing the songs and imagining the crowds a few years from then, listening to my songs.

One night, I had a dream where I was standing atop the world's most famous stage. I could hear the audience cheering, clapping, and singing along to my music. I woke with a fire inside me, knowing that my dream would come true one day.

I remember getting involved in a community by working with the members of the Seventh-Day Adventist Church, which included The Adventure Club and Pathfinder Club created by the Seventh-day Adventist Church (SDA). I was eager to learn more about the club's origin and many other lessons that would help as a young girl growing up in her faith. The club enabled me to develop a skill for leading group songs and taking charge of other tasks I will be asked to do.

The church was an extraordinary place for the local community. Every Sabbath, people from all walks of life came to experience the warm embrace of the Almighty. But it wasn't just on the Sabbath that the church had a reach; the youth clubs they held on Saturdays were just as important as the other days.

The youth clubs allowed the community to learn about God and grow their spirituality. It was an authentic learning experience facilitated by qualified teachers and ministers.

However, the youth clubs were not just about religious education; the church members believed in a holistic approach to learning, so the club members were taken on field trips to learn new skills and strengthen their social ties to the local community.

Many youths who attended the club became a part of the local economy by doing Gospel music, youth ministry, and activism for social change. This was all made possible because of the door that the church opened for them to the world. It was a significant blessing in every sense of the word.

The church will always be remembered for its positive impact on its youth members and all those who looked up to it as a center for faith and knowledge.

> The church has youth clubs where children learn and gain knowledge of God and real-life skills.

I started to get more engaged in children's programs called "The Adventure Club" and "Pathfinder Club," created by the Seventh-day Adventist Church (SDA) at the age of 4 to 13. During my involvement in club programs, I discovered more about myself and the talent that I am naturally born with; this includes singing, drawing, and other potential skills that would help me later in life. I am passionate about singing. This made me write songs and express the words of the Bible in my songs to the audience. I hoped to sing and touch the hearts of others and spread the message of God. Aside from all the other things I love, I considered singing a part of my joy and inspiring journey, where I also wanted to help others navigate a positive side of life.

I was so pleased that I just wanted to do more of what I enjoyed and felt when I sang. I started to be more active in the club's activities, where I could prove my singing skills with other personal skills. And that's precisely what I did.

Through the Seventh-day Adventist Church (SDA) Clubs, I had thus discovered the potential talent I had. Singing quickly became one of my most loved hobbies and passions. I even thought of becoming a professional singer one day.

Back to church, there were many different levels of club with its age range. As for me, I transfer from Adventure Club to another. After reaching 12, I moved to another club called the Pathfinder Club at Kigamboni Seventh Day Church. It was an exciting transition, as I was eager to explore new activities and make new friends. The club's tradition of hosting various events and activities throughout the year kept us engaged and motivated.

Every afternoon, after attending church, we would gather for club meetings to practice our programs. The atmosphere was always enthusiastic as we prepared for upcoming events.

We would spend hours rehearsing our Pathfinder parade, which required precision and coordination. The leaders would guide us, ensuring that our formations were flawless and our movements were synchronized.

Aside from the parade, we also focused on learning about the history of Pathfinders, acquiring life skills and survival techniques, and understanding biblical concepts relevant to the day's topic. Sunday afternoons were dedicated to intensive practice sessions, where we delved deep into these subjects. It was a practical and interactive way of learning, making the sessions both educational and enjoyable.

One of the highlights of being a part of the Pathfinder Club was attending camps. These camps allowed us to connect with nature, learn outdoor skills, and bond with our fellow club members. We would spend days hiking, setting tents, and cooking meals. These experiences taught me self-reliance and teamwork and instilled a love for nature. The memories made during these camps will forever hold a special place in my heart.

Looking back on my journey, I am grateful for the Pathfinders who have participated in it. From the leaders who patiently mentored us to the friends who shared countless laughs and joy, each person significantly shaped my character and values. The club provided me with a platform to showcase my talents and skills and taught me valuable life lessons that I carry today.

As I grow and mature, I look back at my time in the Pathfinder Club with fondness and gratitude. It was an invaluable chapter in my life, where I honed my abilities, nurtured lifelong friendships, and embraced the club's core principles. The lessons and experiences gained have enriched my personal and professional journey, making me a better individual.

The Pathfinder Club holds a special place in my heart, as it has left an indelible mark on my life. Its impact on my growth and development is immeasurable, and I am forever grateful for the opportunity to be a part of such a wonderful organization. As I look forward to new adventures and challenges, I carry the spirit of the Pathfinder Club with me, cherishing the memories and the lessons learned along the way.

***

The municipal council of Kigamboni was abuzz with activities. I sat in a quiet corner of one of the buildings as the club members gathered around me after noticing how calm I was all the time. I was known for my enigmatic silence – a whisper in a crowd, a quiet presence at social gatherings.

"Why don't you speak?" one of the club members finally mustered the courage to ask, expressing the curiosity that had been simmering within them for so long.

I looked up as our eyes locked onto the interested member. A subtle smirk tugged at the corner of my lips as if I relished the opportunity to reveal my secret. With a dramatic pause, I leaned in closer, the rest of the club leaning in with bated breath.

"Shhh," I whispered, my voice like velvet caressing their ears, "secrets whispered are secrets kept."

Confusion washed over the club members, their brows furrowing in perplexity. They thought they had finally uncovered the mystery, yet it seemed to deepen further.

"But why?" another club member stammered, desperate for answers.

A teenage girl, I chuckled softly, a fascinating sound that seemed to carry a mystical aura. I leaned back, my eyes gleaming mischievously.

"Why should I speak when silence says so much more?" I murmured, casting a mysterious glance around the room.

"Sometimes the quiet ones hold the greatest power in a world of noise."

With that cryptic declaration, I rose from my seat and gracefully walked away, leaving the club members unconcerned in my wake.

And so, the enigma of the silent teenager continued to confound those who encountered me, leaving them with unresolved questions and a sense of intrigue that would linger for years to come.

Intrigue echoed through the room as I disappeared, leaving the club members yearning for answers but knowing deep down that some secrets were meant to be kept.

A glimmer of understanding swept across their faces as they pondered this thought. They realized there was more to this silent mystery than meets the eye.

Thus, their journey to unravel the enigmatic silence as I began while they delved into my past and sought the truth hidden within my silent lips.

***

As a teenage girl, I always approached things methodically, taking them one step at a time and figuring out what to do next. I was a quiet teen and found solace within myself, where I could gather all the necessary information to develop and grow through different stages of my life. While I learned how to engage with other kids, my innate nature often contradicted my efforts. I found it challenging to fit in with others, but I always did my best to mingle with them so they would feel included and included. Despite the difficulties, I persisted and tried my hardest.

Growing up, my inclination towards introspection and analysis shaped my worldview. I would spend countless hours contemplating life's mysteries, learning about various subjects, and discovering who I was. This approach allowed me to develop a deep understanding and a unique perspective on the world.

My reserved nature sometimes made it difficult for me to make friends in school. I struggled to find common ground with my peers, who seemed to navigate social situations effortlessly. However, I refused to let this hinder my personal growth. I pushed myself to engage in conversations, participate in group activities, and step out of my comfort zone.

Over time, I realized that my introversion was not a flaw but a strength. It enabled me to observe and listen attentively to others, understanding their perspectives and building deep connections. While others might perceive my reserved nature as aloof, I knew it reflected my contemplative disposition.

My passion for knowledge and self-discovery eventually led me toward immersing myself in the world and research. As I delved deeper into my activities, the quiet girl who struggled to fit in with her peers transformed into a confident and knowledgeable individual.

Through my journey, I learned to embrace my introversion and use it to my advantage. It became my instrument to connect with people on a meaningful level. Although I may not have been the spirited life of the party, I discovered a quiet strength within myself that commanded attention and respect.

Reflecting on my past, I am grateful for the challenges I faced during my childhood. They instilled a sense of perseverance and taught me the value of authenticity. My journey from a reserved and quiet child to a confident and self-assured individual has been transformative.

Throughout my journey, I aim to inspire others who share similar experiences. Everyone has their unique journey, and it is in embracing our individuality that we can truly thrive. Our quiet nature should not be seen as a hindrance but as a guiding light towards self-discovery and inner strength.

And as I continue to navigate life, I carry the valuable lessons learned from my introverted childhood. I embrace my nature, cherishing the moments of solitude that allow me to recharge and delve deeper into my inner world. I am grateful for the person I have become, and I eagerly look forward to the next chapter of my story, knowing that I will continue to grow, learn, and inspire others along the way.

At the same time, in my personal life, music had always been a passionate and powerful force in my life, so even though my schoolwork and personal obligations had taken me away from it for a few decades, it never entirely left me. At first, I just sang for fun, but soon, I felt the urge to take it more seriously, allow myself to be vulnerable, and expose my raw emotions through lyrics and melody.

Maybe it was a different kind of calling, a way for God to reach out to me and take me down a more fulfilling path. I started writing my songs and performing them daily and around my area, where I would find a small place to practice and sing them; my faith and the power of music intermingled to an incredible effect.

The performance results I got from people close to me or my peers were so powerful and humbling that it made me realize this was the part of my life I wanted to pursue. I hoped to touch the hearts of others and spread the message of God through my music, to embrace and lift them with lyrics of faith and joy, to take people on a spiritual journey, and to help them bridge the gap between their dreams and realities. That's why, when I perform, I always want my music to have a lasting impact on those who listen. I wanted to create an atmosphere of peace and understanding— a place to find solace and strength. I continue to write and perform my music to make it a personal expression of faith and a source of comfort and community.

> Music had always been a passionate and powerful force in my life, so even though my schoolwork and personal obligations had taken me away from it for a few decades, it never entirely left me.

I was finally taking the plunge. I had been wishing, hoping, and planning to start singing for months. Every night, I visualized my dream come true, but until today, my courage mustered itself.

One step at a time was my mantra as I took my first step forward.

It was challenging for me. I was scared, my palms sweating, my anxiety bubbling up. I had worked hard for months to make things a reality but had an ache to do something independently. Now that I had finally taken the plunge, the excitement was beginning to replace the anxiousness.

The next few weeks were challenging and overwhelming, but I powered through. I was determined to make my dream a reality. I took updated courses, crafted my singing plan, picked a great location, and started working on the process. My vision became more accurate with each step forward.

One step at a time was a motto that had served me well before I started to see my dream become a reality.

And by cultivating love and faith in music, I hoped to inspire others to discover the beauty of their journey and to build up those around them. I was driven by a deep conviction that Music is a powerful tool for good, and I wanted to use it to share the divine message of God.

I had always known what I wanted out of life, but I never knew exactly what steps to take to reach there. So, to reach my goals, I planned on a path of self-discovery and determination.

I wrote down my dreams, examined my motivations, and listed my resources. I knew that if I wanted to achieve my goals, I would have to take it step by step, but I also had to be open to the unknown and become flexible if needed.

I became aware that this would be a long journey, and there were moments when I felt lost. But I repeated to myself every night by saying trusting the process. I trusted that everything I'd finished would eventually get me where I wanted to be.

I continue to remind myself as I was continuously being driven by a deep conviction that Music is a powerful tool for good and want to use it to share the divine message of God. I began to believe that there was more to life than what I am currently doing.

I stuck to my route and kept taking steps forward no matter what. Things were sometimes unclear, but I knew that finishing each degree would lead to the next and eventually to my goal.

And sure enough, over time, my efforts paid off. After months of dedicating my time, energy, and resources, I achieved one of my goals. I couldn't believe what I had accomplished and felt proud of myself for staying focused and not giving up when everything seemed hazy.

I realized it was worth following the process, one step at a time, even when the endpoint seemed unknown.

I was always surrounded by simplicity and a close-knit community. Life seemed easy, predictable, and secure. But as I embarked on my journey to discover more about myself and my personal growth, I quickly learned that life is anything but unpredictable.

My early years of childhood were filled with dreams of greatness. I had big ambitions and aspired to achieve extraordinary things. However, I often found myself overwhelmed by the enormity of my goals. Doubt would creep in, and I would question whether I could genuinely realize my aspirations.

During these moments of uncertainty, I turned to trusting the process. I realized that life is not meant to be rushed; it is a journey that unfolds step by step. By embracing this mindset, I could let go of my fears and trust in the path before me.

This newfound perspective gave me a clear vision of how things would unfold. I was no longer obsessed over the result but focused on each small victory. I celebrated every milestone, no matter how insignificant it may have seemed. Each step forward brought me closer to my goal.

As I navigated through life, I encountered countless challenges and obstacles. There were moments when I wanted to give up and succumb to mediocrity's comfort. But I reminded myself of the power of God and pressed on.

Through adversity, I discovered my true strengths and capabilities. I realized that setbacks were not signs of failure but rather growth opportunities. Rather than dwelling on my mistakes or misfortunes, I learned to embrace them and extract valuable lessons from each experience.

Trusting the process became my guiding principle. It allowed me to remain focused and determined, even when circumstances presented themselves as insurmountable. I learned to stay patient and adapt to the ever-changing nature of life.

As a young teenage girl, I possessed an insatiable curiosity and an indomitable spirit, constantly yearning to uncover the purpose of my existence. As I journeyed to discover God's will for my life, I contemplated the weighty concept of the divine will.

Growing up in a pious household, I was always taught the importance of trusting God's plan. However, as I entered my teenage years, questions began to surface within my seeking mind, urging me to seek clarity about my purpose.

AMID MY QUESTIONABLE EXISTENCE

I started with introspection and prayer to discover who I am. I spent countless nights pondering the meaning of my life and seeking guidance from the mighty God. I delved deep into religious texts, seeking solace and wisdom to quell my unrest. With each passing day, my desire to understand God's will grew more robust, and I knew it was a path I had to undertake.

In my quest for divine guidance, I sought the mentorship of knowledgeable individuals who could offer insights and perspectives beyond my limited understanding. I engaged in thoughtful discussions with spiritual leaders, seeking answers to myriad questions in my head. Their patience and wisdom gave me a new perspective on God's will.

During this journey, I learned that God's will is not a predetermined, fixed path for us. It is not a one-size-fits-all approach to life. God's will be deeply personal and unique to everyone. It is a delicate balance between our desires, aspirations, and the guidance and wisdom from a mighty God.

I also realized that discovering God's will is not a one-time but an ongoing process. As we grow and evolve, so does our understanding of our purpose in life. It requires constant self-reflection, prayer, and an open heart to discern the subtle signs and guidance that God provides.

Throughout this journey, I grappled with moments of doubt and uncertainty. I questioned whether my search for purpose a worthy pursuit was or just a fruitless endeavor. But deep down, I knew that unanswered questions were not signs of a lack of faith but rather an opportunity for growth and a deeper connection with God.

As I navigated the tumultuous waters of adolescence, I discovered that the true essence of God's will lies in the journey itself. In moments of doubt and questioning, we find our strength and resilience. We uncover our true purpose and calling through introspection and self-reflection.

The road to understanding God's will is not always smooth and often fraught with challenges and setbacks. But in those obstacles, we find the lessons necessary for our growth and self-discovery. We unlock the doors to our true potential by embracing the unknown and trusting in God's providence.

Throughout my teenage years, I am grateful for the questions that once plagued my mind. They pushed me to embark on a journey to discover who I am and to seek a deeper connection with God. Though my understanding of God will continue to evolve, I am comforted by the knowledge that my purpose in life is not predetermined but rather a sacred partnership between my aspirations and the divine guidance I seek.

Looking back, I am grateful for the transformation that occurred within me. Trusting the process not only enabled me to achieve my goals but also allowed me to discover who I truly am. It taught me resilience in the face of adversity and instilled in me a sense of purpose.

Today, as I reflect upon my journey, I can proudly say that I have accomplished more than I ever thought possible. But what I value most is not the result but the person I have become. Each step of my historical life has been a testament to the power of trusting God, resilience, and personal growth.

CHAPTER 3

WHAT IS MY CALLING? IS IT THE ONE?

It was a hot summer morning in 2012 when my parents dropped me off at the gates of Main Green Hill Secondary School. As the car pulled away, my heart sank, and tears filled my eyes. Even though it had been months since I was accepted to boarding school, I was still not ready to leave the comfort of my home and family behind.

I exited the car and slowly went to the entrance with my parents. My luggage felt heavy in my hands, and my throat was tight with emotion. I felt a wave of homesickness wash over me as I entered the unfamiliar halls of my new school. I was scared and unsure of what lay ahead, but I knew I had to face it bravely and guard my innermost feelings.

I was given a tour of the school by the matron, a school tour guide, and shown to my dormitory room. I was given the basic instructions on how to get around the school and complete my studies. Before I joined the matron, I hugged my mother and said goodbye to her as I held my tears from rolling down my face. Then, it was time for everyone to move on to their respective activities. My mom used to come occasionally to see me, and then there was this one last visit where my mother came to check on my well-being. I remember going to the principal's office with my mother as the school's headmaster told her, "Madam, don't come to visit her frequently; she'll be unable to adjust to her new environment. Let her get used to the environment and experience being away from home. Otherwise, she'll end up not being able to adjust." Later, my mom said goodbye to me after we left the office. She said, "Study well, my daughter." Well, it's safe to say it worked! I began to train myself not to remember anything related to home and began to enjoy my new home at boarding school.

As the hours passed and I got to know the other students, I slowly settled into life at boarding school. The days were filled with studying, socializing, and participating in extracurricular activities. But every night before I would go to bed, I would stand at the window of my room and look out at the night sky. I knew it would not be forever and that this would all be a distant memory soon.

Looking back now, I realize that going to boarding school was one of the best experiences of my life. It taught me to appreciate what I have and gave me the confidence to take on anything. And the day my parents sent me to board school, Main Green Hill Secondary School, was a defining moment, and I will never forget it.

Being set away to boarding school was the happiest and saddest day of my life. On the one hand, I was ecstatic to finally be on my own and away from parental influence. On the other hand, I was defeated by the realization that I was no closer to knowing what to do with my life than when I first arrived.

I felt like an insignificant speck in a much larger machine at Main Green Hill Secondary School. Everyone around me seemed to know where they were going in life. My lack of certainty about my future felt more daunting than ever before.

To make matters worse, I was surrounded by individuals who could relate to my uncertainty. These young adults had many worries about the constraints of the traditional college and job path. I felt like I was the only one who didn't have concrete plans.

Ultimately, attending boarding school showed me I was not alone. The people around me were in the same place I was. Despite their fears and insecurities, seeing how determined they were to create something rewarding for themselves was inspiring.

Through the support of my peers, I was able to come to terms with my feelings of insecurity and anxiety. I learned there is no rush to figure out what to do with my life. Instead, I learned to take it one day at a time and enjoy my journey.

One night, after coming out of the assembly for evening devotion, our matron, as I liked to call her, was an older woman who had overseen the dorms for decades. She was eccentric, always wearing colorful clothes and telling stories about her exciting past. But I also noticed the wisdom in her eyes and the kindness in her demeanor.

One day, after classes were done, I had a terrible day. I felt like everyone around me was the same, but I was different. I didn't know what to do, so I asked myself, "Should I go to the matron's office?" As I was about to make my final decision, she came, "Rachel, is everything okay?" I told the matron and answered her, pretending everything was okay. "Yes, I am. Thank you for asking." Her asking me a question was enough for me.

The matron smiled and enveloped me in a hug. "It's okay, everything will be alright, you're special, don't worry," she said. "Everyone has their paths in life, and that's something to be celebrated."

I felt the warmth of my matron's embrace and was comforted by her words. I felt a newfound courage rising in me.

I stayed in boarding school, embracing my uniqueness. With the matron's encouraging words and friendship, I found my way to success. "It's okay, everything is good," I would tell myself, feeling confident.

And I always remembered those kind words from my dormitory matron.

It was another sleepy afternoon at boarding school as the sun lazily streamed through the windows. As a new student who just transferred not long ago, I sighed, my weary eyes fixated on the worn-out dormitory door beside me. I was lost in my thoughts when a soft voice abruptly pierced the silence. I looked up at the blue sky, my eyes filled with hope. I felt a little lonely as I was new and not knowing anybody, longing for a connection that seemed just out of reach. One day, as I gazed at the clouds, I thought: what if I could become someone's little sister?

"Mm Hi there." A petite girl with big, innocent eyes came into view, wearing a Persian and dark green school uniform that was part of our second clothes to wear aside from our official school uniform... "Can I become your big sister?" she asked, timid and hopeful.

Caught off guard as a student, I blinked with surprise. "Um...sure, I suppose. But why?"

The older girl's gaze softened. I understood the yearning for familial connection. After all, I had often felt alone in this bustling place. With a warm smile, I patted the spot beside her and said, "Of course you can! Welcome to the sisterhood!"

The older girl's face lit up with joy as she plopped beside her newfound little sister. We exchanged stories, laughter, and secrets as we sat, forging a bond that neither of us had imagined possible.

And so, in the quiet embrace of that dormitory door, a glimpse of hope blossomed as we both found solace in our shared sisterhood.

Winds of laughter and love danced through our hearts, filling our world with warmth and possibility. Little did we know that this newfound bond would forever change our lives.

I was beginning my first year at Secondary School. Everything felt new and intimidating, from the more prominent buildings and students to the looming expectations of the upper-level students. My only comfort was the kind dorm that would be my matron for the rest of the academic year at Main Green Hill.

On my first day of orientation, the school's matron welcomed the new students with an uplifting and reassuring speech: "It's okay to be different from others."

The words resonated with me; I felt like I would stand out. Everything from my dress style to my interests made me different from the other students. Already, I could feel the whispers as people speculated why I was wearing those clothes or carrying those books.

I took the matron's advice to heart and embraced her differences. I refused to hide my unusual hobbies or suppress my unique thoughts. The Matron noticed my newfound confidence and was proud of my growth.

As a young student, I started a new term at Main Green Hill Secondary School. I was excited but also a little anxious. I was used to roaming around places with my family during weekends and on special occasions but never had to experience a formal education and disciplinary structure.

***

While studying at Main Green Hill Secondary School, I never imagined that I would encounter one of the familiar faces I had known from my days at Diamond International Primary

School. Seeing Francisca, a young lady I had known all those years ago, was quite a surprise. She was in Form Four then, whereas I had just started Form One. It was incredible to think that our paths would cross again.

When Francisca and I spotted each other that day, our faces lit up with happiness. We greeted each other warmly, exchanging stories about our lives since we had last met. We couldn't help but marvel at the coincidence of bumping into one another at this new school. It honestly reminded us of how small the world can be.

As we caught up, memories from our primary school days flooded back. It was the year of 2008 when she graduated from 7th grade, and I was in grade four at that time. Francisca had always been a bright, diligent student, and it was no surprise that she excelled academically. She aspired to pursue a career of her choice and was already working towards fulfilling that dream.

On the other hand, I had taken a different path. I was drawn to the arts and developed a passion for creative writing. While my academic pursuits were necessary, I also focused on exploring my creative side by participating in school plays, volunteering, and after-school activities.

Over time, Francisca and I became good friends again, supporting each other in our respective endeavors. We realized that even though we had taken different paths, we still shared a deep bond of friendship. Francisca's determination and focus inspired me to work harder in my studies, while my creativity sparked her interest in exploring different ways to express herself.

Through our interactions, we discovered that studying at the same school again allowed us to grow together in many ways. Our different perspectives and interests enriched our friendship, and we learned daily from each other.

I am grateful for the unexpected reunion with Francisca. Our friendship endured and flourished, contributing to our personal growth and success. As we embarked on our different journeys, we carried with us the memories of our encounters and the lessons we learned from each other.

I realized that, indeed, life is full of surprises, and you never know who you may encounter again in the future. Francisca's reappearance in my life reminded me that our connections are not limited by time or distance. The world truly is a small place, and these chance encounters make each step of our journey even more meaningful.

The first few weeks were filled with trepidation. I slowly adjusted to the school lifestyle, attending assemblies, sitting in class, and meeting new people. One of the most challenging tasks I faced was attending school activities.

Surprisingly, the students welcomed me and encouraged me to join in. I decided to take the plunge, joined the youth choir, helped the Pastor lead the evening worship before studying during night prep, and volunteered for the school community. It was a steep learning curve, but I persevered.

Every Saturday, I will see myself standing in front of the youth choir, singing loudly and enthusiastically. Seeing the other student's faces light up gave me a sense of belonging and purpose.

The final big challenge was giving a public speech. I remember my Pastor told me days before Saturday to preach during worship. "Rachel, would you mind leading the sermon on Saturday?" Without hesitation, I said, "Yes". I got nervous at first; then, I began to search for a topic to cover. I prayed and asked God to help me prepare the case. Then Matthew 24 came to mind. Soon, the day finally arrived. I plucked up the courage and spoke to the students. I remember we were at the school hall when I first presented my first public speech. Everyone was highly impressed with my articulateness and knowledge. This is where I finally found my place in the school and, more importantly, in my heart.

I learned that even when I was most anxious and uncertain, I could quickly become comfortable and find a place where I belonged. It was empowering and an experience I would cherish for years to come.

One of the most surprising things about my studying at Main Green Hill is that it was straightforward for me to be found, all due to my physical appearance. If someone is looking for me, they would ask the students questions like "Where is Rachel?" or "Did you see Rachel by any chance?" Well, that would give you an immediate answer to where I was located.

***

What is my calling? Is it the one? As a teenage girl trying to figure out God's call in my life. It was a question that lingered in my mind day and night, keeping me restless and filled with doubt. Growing up in a religious household, I was taught from a young age about the importance of following God's plan for my life. But as I reached my teenage years, I wondered if I was truly living up to my purpose.

I attended sabbath school faithfully, listened to sermons attentively, and even participated in various church activities. However, deep down, I felt a nagging sense of inadequacy. I watched my peers excelling in different areas with their talents and gifts and wondered why I couldn't find my calling.

As a young teenage girl, I could sense that there were always signs that God had a calling on my life, a destiny in store for me and that there was more to it. However, I needed to thoroughly understand the assignment and what it looked like.

To trust the process, I discovered writing songs and began to see a glimmer of hope. As I poured my thoughts and emotions onto paper, I realized that this could be the medium through which I would discover my purpose. I started penning stories, poems, and essays, finding solace and fulfillment in the power of words.

With encouragement from my parents and teachers, I pursued my passion for writing. I joined the creative writing club in high school and participated in local writing competitions. Each accolade fueled my ambition and strengthened my resolve to continue this path.

However, doubts still lingered. Was writing my calling? Could I truly make a difference in the world through my words? The uncertainty and fear of failure often left me questioning whether I was on the right track.

As I continued my secondary education, I studied various subjects, including Physics, Chemistry, Biology, English, creative writing, etc. The curriculum exposed me to various literary works and allowed me to experiment with different writing styles. Through the guidance of passionate professors, I honed my skills and learned to express myself more effectively.

I began to sense a deeper purpose behind my writing during this time. I could shed light on important issues through storytelling, evoke empathy, and inspire change. Words held the power to heal, to ignite revolutions, and to give voice to the voiceless. I realized that my calling wasn't just about writing for my fulfillment but using the written word as a tool for transformation.

With newfound clarity, I began to look for other ways to re-imagine myself writing for a particular cause that aligned with my passion. I envision myself writing for non-profit organizations and advocating for causes close to my heart, and I started to see the impact my words could have. Through these experiences, I realized I was living out God's purpose for my life, one term at a time.

Today, as I reflect upon my journey, I am grateful for the doubts and uncertainties that propelled me toward my calling. They forced me to question, dig deep, and ultimately find my true purpose. Life may still hold challenges and moments of doubt, but I am confident in my chosen path.

"What is my calling? Is it the one?" This little girl's question has finally been answered. Through writing, I have found my purpose in life and am determined to continue making a difference, one word at a time.

As a Main Green Hill Secondary School student, I felt stirred up by something inside me.

I couldn't understand the feeling, but eventually, it clicked. I later knew that the Holy Spirit was moving in my heart to call me to something greater. My mind started filling up with the words and melody of the song "Kufungwa Kwa Mlango wa Rehema," inspired by my vision of the future God had for me.

That night, I grabbed my notebook and pen and started to piece together the lyrics and melody for Kufungwa Kwa Mlango wa Rehema. I wrote of a distant future, of a journey full of joy and hope, and of a place of rest I understood was to be my destiny. When I had finished writing the song, I knew there was something special about it and that the Lord was calling me to something.

When I sang Kufungwa Kwa Mlango wa Rehema alone around the school campus the next day, I was blown away by how good the song appeared. It was a powerful, bittersweet song about courage and believing in the future despite the present hardship. We all committed to supporting each other in whatever journey the Lord had for us.

Since then, I've been blessed with the opportunity of a lifetime - to pursue my dreams of making music and impacting the world. Through it all, I've remembered to trust in the Lord and allow the Holy Spirit to lead me. Kufungwa Kwa Mlango wa Rehema will always remind me of that calling and my journey.

Looking back, when I was a little girl, I often felt lost and confused trying to navigate life. I couldn't help but wonder what God wanted from me, and I questioned if He had any particular purpose for my life.

The Sunday morning sun shone brightly as I sat alone on a bench inside the boarding school at the school dining hall, deep in my thoughts. The weight of my worries dragged me down, threatening to suffocate me. But then, out of nowhere, a voice pierced through the silence.

"Hey, you are there! Mind if I join you?"

I turned my head to see a cheerful girl approaching me. Her vibrant energy radiated from her, instantly brightening up my gloomy surroundings.

She is plopping down on the bench beside me without waiting for my response. "What's your name?"

Surprised by her courageous approach, I blinked but couldn't help but laugh. "I'm Rachel," I replied. It seemed fitting, given the situation.

She grinned, her eyes twinkling with mischief. "Oh, I like that. Together, on this sunny morning. Sounds like the start of a great adventure!"

A mix of curiosity and amusement washed over me. "What do you mean?"

She leaned closer, whispering conspiratorially. "You see, Rachel, I believe that even in the darkest times, there's always a glimpse of hope. We have to be brave enough to find it."

Her words resonated within me, piercing through the clouds of doubt that had consumed me. At that moment, excitement ignited in my soul, breathing life into my weary spirit.

A gust of wind rustled the leaves overhead like nature was cheering us on. I laughed again, feeling a newfound sense of optimism. "Alright, I'm ready for this adventure. Show me the way to that glimpse of hope."

She raised her hands, her laughter echoing through the crisp morning air. "Hold on tight, Rachel, because we're about to embark on a journey unlike anything you've ever experienced!"

And with that, we stood together, ready to face whatever lay ahead. As we walked hand in hand, I couldn't help but feel a sense of anticipation building within me. This glimpse of hope could be enough to change everything.

Little did I know my life was about to take an unexpected turn, which would lead me down a path I never could have imagined. But for now, all I had to do was hold on, smile, and believe in the power of God.

***

One evening at church, after I left school for a break, I was inspired by the pastor's sermon. He spoke about the importance of listening to the still, small voice within and discovering God's call and purpose for each person. When he finished, I decided to journey to find God's call and purpose for my life.

I took a few days off from my routine and committed to spending time in nature. I will go out for a short walk, stopping often to sit and meditate on my purpose. As I walked, I prayed for guidance and a sign that God had an intention for my life.

I've been a Christian all my life, but until recently, I lived a relatively unfocused life. I had to go to school, be around friends, and get involved in my hobbies, but nothing had given me the sense of purpose I had been searching for.

One day, while praying, I felt God calling me to do something more with my life. I didn't know what it was, but I was determined to find out.

I began to read the Bible more regularly and attended weekly Bible studies at my local church. I also started praying, asking God to reveal His purpose for my life.

One night, while praying, I heard a small voice prompting me to start a ministry in my community. I was filled with a sense of excitement and purpose. I knew this was what God was calling me to do. However, I didn't know what shape or form it would take yet, but I was sure of my purpose and calling. Some people told me that I should start singing. Looking back, it all makes sense. I had gone on my journey to discover God's call for my life and found it. Finally, I was ready to start the next stage of my journey and embrace my God-given destiny.

I often found solace in attending Children's Sabbath School as a young child. The stories of bravery, faith, and divine intervention fascinated me. Despite my tender age, I longed to know what purpose lay ahead. It became a burning desire within my heart, and as the years passed, I knew that my search for God's call was inevitable.

Each day, I sought guidance and understanding through prayer and meditation. I sought wisdom from those who had traveled this path before me, seeking advice from mentors and spiritual leaders who could impart their knowledge. Armed with their insights, I focused on self-reflection, tirelessly exploring my passions, talents, and aspirations.

Through the trials and triumphs, I discovered that my true purpose lay in service to others. I sensed my calling pulsating, urging me to bring light and hope to those who needed it most. With a renewed sense of clarity, my career turned towards humanitarian work, leading me to remote corners of the world where suffering and injustice clouded the lives of countless individuals.

For years, I toiled in the trenches, dedicating my time, energy, and resources to uplift the lives of those less fortunate. I built schools, provided medical aid, and offered a helping hand wherever needed. It wasn't always easy, but knowing I was fulfilling God's call filled my heart with an unwavering determination to press on.

Amid my noble endeavors, I encountered countless incredible individuals, each with their own stories of struggle and resilience. Their experiences reminded me of the strength of the human spirit and the power of faith. Their unwavering hope and joy in the face of adversity inspired me to continue my mission of extending love and compassion to all those in need.

Each step of my journey brought me closer to understanding the depth of God's love and purpose for my life. Through serving others, I discovered the profound joy, fulfillment, and peace that can only be found when one embraces their God-given calling.

As I continued to reflect on the chapters of my life, I was grateful for the winding road that led me to this moment. The trials and tribulations, the joys and sorrows, have shaped me into a person from the present time. With a heart brimming with gratitude, I stood at the precipice of my destiny, ready to embrace the next stage of my journey.

I stepped into the unknown with unwavering faith and an indomitable spirit, trusting that God would continue guiding and empowering me. As I continue to learn more and understand the will of God in my life, I am resolute in my commitment to fulfill it. The world awaits, and I am ready to make a difference, one life at a time.

It was a personal journey and a testament to the power of faith, resilience, and obedience to God's calling. It is a reminder that, within each of us, the potential for greatness and the ability to impact the world meaningfully. I am humbled and honored to embark on this next chapter, seeking to fulfill the purpose for which I was created as I embrace my God-given destiny with open arms.

… AMID MY QUESTIONABLE EXISTENCE

CHAPTER 4

THE DEBUT OF MY FIRST ALBUM

It was the evening of 2012 when the students went to the cafeteria to eat dinner.... I was in the dormitory lying down for half of the day, feeling helpless, and I didn't know what was wrong with me after fainting three times in a row. I remember my roommates surrounded me on the side of the bed, including Rebecca, Halima, Pendo, and other students, to check up on me to see if there was any progress. My matron came to see me, the pastor came to pray for me, and the coordinator and headmaster decided to call for my parents to pick me up. I didn't know that was the last time I would ever be in school and be able to see my friends.

My dad came to school and parked the car closer to where my dormitory was located and saw my luggage being put in the trunk. It was an emotional moment for me and my other friend as they said goodbye while lying inside the car before leaving.

After I moved out of boarding school in 2012 to study closer to home so that my parents could monitor my health, I took the rest of the months off from school before I began my studies the following year. My parents registered me at the school named Tungi Secondary School, which was one block away from home. The school was located near Kigamboni SDA Church across the road.

In the following months after moving out of boarding school, I began to attend hospital visits. I went from one hospital to another to find out what was happening inside my body or if there was anything serious that was bothering me. I went on and did all kinds of checkups, you can name it, from MIR, CT SCAN, to Chest X-rays, and so on. None of the treatments show any sickness. As for myself, I began to question myself: why has it all happened to me? I began to look for answers to the questions I had in my mind.

My parents began to put me in prayers, and people from church also began to pray for me, from elders to pastors and congregations. Even those I didn't know also joined me in prayer. I also began to attend other SDA churches outside of the district region from where I currently lived to participate in weekly prayer sessions. We sought answers to the problem and asked God for His divine intervention.

The situation was worse than I imagined, meaning I could drop anywhere. I would always be accompanied by family members anywhere except for school. I remember one of the elders from church came to visit early in the morning, around 7 Am or 8 Am, because I could see the sunrise to pray for me as I lay on my bed. Mr. Steven M. introduced me to the book of Psalm 35 and told me to pray this bible verse daily. The funny thing is that I began to form it into a song and memorized it so I could sing it anytime.

Psalm 35:1-28 New King James Version (NKJV).

The Lord the Avenger of His People.

<u>A Psalm of David.</u>

35 Plead my cause, O Lord, with those who

strive with me;

Fight against those who fight against me.

² Take hold of shield and buckler,

And stand up for my help.

³ Also draw out the spear,

And stop those who pursue me.

Say to my soul,

"I am your salvation."

AMID MY QUESTIONABLE EXISTENCE

⁴ Let those be put to shame and brought to dishonor
Who seek after my life;
Let those be turned back and brought to confusion
Who plot my hurt.
⁵ Let them be like chaff before the wind,
And let the angel of the Lord chase them.
⁶ Let their way be dark and slippery,
And let the angel of the Lord pursue them.
⁷ For without cause they have hidden their net for me in a pit,
Which they have dug without cause for my life.
⁸ Let destruction come upon him unexpectedly,
And let his net that he has hidden catch himself;
Into that very destruction let him fall.

AMID MY QUESTIONABLE EXISTENCE

⁹ And my soul shall be joyful in the Lord;

It shall rejoice in His salvation.

¹⁰ All my bones shall say,

"Lord, who is like You,

Delivering the poor from him who is too strong

for him,

Yes, the poor and the needy from him who

plunders him?"

¹¹ Fierce witnesses rise up;

They ask me things that I do not know.

¹² They reward me evil for good,

To the sorrow of my soul.

¹³ But as for me, when they were sick,

My clothing was sackcloth;

I humbled myself with fasting;

And my prayer would return to my own heart.

¹⁴ I paced about as though he were my

AMID MY QUESTIONABLE EXISTENCE

friend or brother;

I bowed down heavily, as one who mourns for hismother.

{sup}15{/sup} But in my [g]adversity they rejoiced

And gathered together;

Attackers gathered against me,

And I did not know it;

They tore at me and did not cease;

{sup}16{/sup} With ungodly mockers at feasts

They gnashed at me with their teeth.

{sup}17{/sup} Lord, how long will You look on?

Rescue me from their destructions,

My precious life from the lions.

{sup}18{/sup} I will give You thanks in the great assembly;

I will praise You among many people.

{sup}19{/sup} Let them not rejoice over me who are wrongfully my enemies;

Nor let them wink with the eye who hate me

without a cause.

[20] For they do not speak peace,

But they devise deceitful matters

Against the quiet ones in the land.

[21] They also opened their mouth wide against

me,

And said, "Aha, aha!

Our eyes have seen it."

[22] This You have seen, O Lord;

Do not keep silence.

O Lord, do not be far from me.

[23] Stir up Yourself, and awake to my vindication,

To my cause, my God and my Lord.

[24] Vindicate me, O Lord my God, according to

Your righteousness;

And let them not rejoice over me.

*²⁵ Let them not say in their hearts, "Ah, so we
would have it!"*
Let them not say, "We have swallowed him up."
*²⁶ Let them be ashamed and brought to mutual
confusion*
Who rejoice at my hurt;
Let them be clothed with shame and dishonor
Who exalt themselves against me.
²⁷ Let them shout for joy and be glad,
Who favor my righteous cause;
And let them say continually,
"Let the Lord be magnified,
*Who has pleasure in the prosperity of His
servant."*
*²⁸ And my tongue shall speak of Your
righteousness*
And of Your praise all the day long.

At any moment, I would join the prayer committee at church or home to pray for me. We continue to stay in prayer, hoping for God's intervention.

Then came the year 2013, I felt compelled to do something that tapped into my creative potential - I began writing the songs that would culminate in my first album. Though I had no professional musical experience and felt like I had no skill sets, I took a leap of faith and believed that God would provide a path for me.

I often stayed up late at night, pouring my heart into lyrics and melodies, rewriting and reworking pieces repeatedly until I'd created something I felt proud of. It wasn't just about creating something musically exciting and complex but something that made me feel connected to something larger than myself.

I had always been passionate about music and even wrote some songs. But I only felt I had found my true calling once I discovered writing songs from biblical stories.

I was amazed by how many exciting stories there were to explore, and I quickly set out to write songs that brought these stories to life. I would spend hours researching the stories and trying to find new ways to tell them through music. I wrote songs about Sodom and Gomorrah, the journey to heaven, and many more.

I found that, in writing songs about the bible, I connected with my faith in a deeper and more meaningful way. I could also share my faith with others, as I often performed other songs at church.

It was Saturday afternoon after lunch. I went straight to the choir member who sat under the tree where they usually practice, and I asked the choir teacher to help me create the musical instrument of the songs. Mr. Shangwe asked me, "Do you have the music notes?" I didn't know what he was saying, so he clarified it for me, and I said, "No, Sir, I don't have any keynotes." He said, "Don't worry, we'll go ahead with what you have." I felt so eager to know that everything was starting to fall into place. We will practice the songs individually every Saturday after church on his free schedule.

I wouldn't say my skills and efforts paid off, and it was only by the grace of God that helped me write songs. By 2013, I completed enough pieces for a full album. With the support of my family, it was time for studio and promotion. I remember the excitement and hope I had as I finished the first draft of my album - hopes that it would be well-received and bring joy to others.

The production process was full of highs and lows, but I pushed through, relying on my faith in God and the creative energy of my friends and family. After two years of hard work and dedication, I can proudly say that I did it. I released my first album, and it was a great success. I could promote it and share how God helped me fulfill the task with others. It was a fantastic feeling of fulfillment that I could never have imagined before this journey, and it was the best gift I could've ever asked for.

While creating my music album, I embarked on a journey that would challenge me creatively and personally. As an aspiring artist, I longed to express my deepest emotions and experiences through my music, aiming to touch the hearts of listeners worldwide. Little did I know that this endeavor would require me to rely on a higher power for clarity, wisdom, and guidance.

Each day, I would sit in my makeshift home studio, surrounded by instruments, lyrics scattered across my desk, and the weight of expectation on my shoulders. As I grappled with the magnitude of this project, I found solace in my faith. I turned to God, seeking His guidance and inspiration to craft the profound lyrics defining my album.

The process was challenging. The blank canvases of my mind were filled with fragments of melodies and snippets of words, but weaving them together into coherent, impactful songs proved to be much more trying than I had anticipated. Doubts and insecurities began to creep into my thoughts, threatening to derail my progress.

In those moments of uncertainty, I turned to prayer. I poured out my heart and soul, asking God to grant me clarity and wisdom. I surrendered my creative process to His will, trusting His guidance would lead me to create something extraordinary.

To my surprise, inspiration began to flow. Words danced across the pages as melodies resonated within me, creating a symphony of emotions. It was as if a divine hand was guiding my pen, crafting lines that touched the deepest depths of my being. Each word held meaning; each note carried the weight of my experiences, and I knew something beautiful was emerging from within me.

With each passing day, my reliance on God grew more assertive. I sought His presence before every writing session, humbling myself and acknowledging that my abilities were rooted in a power greater than mine. As I surrendered my ego, my music transformed. It became a vessel through which the divine could speak, carrying messages of love, hope, and resilience.

AMID MY QUESTIONABLE EXISTENCE

As my album neared completion, I realized it was not just a collection of songs but a testament to my faith and the transformative power of God's guidance. Each track carried a piece of my journey, a reflection of my struggles and triumphs, and an invitation for listeners to embark on their spiritual exploration.

Looking back, I am humbled and grateful for the challenges I faced while creating my music album. They tested my perseverance, strengthened my connection with God, and refined my artistry. I now understand that in relying on a power greater than myself, my music became so much more than I could have ever imagined.

Today, as I share my music with the world, I hope others find solace, inspiration, and guidance within its melodies. I trust that the lyrics, crafted with God's wisdom, will touch the hearts of those who listen and remind them of the power of faith in overcoming life's obstacles.

The other kids at school didn't always feel this same enthusiasm for my pursuit of music. They often teased me and told me that singing wastes time and energy. But instead of being discouraged, I held my head high and confidently sang. I was determined to do whatever it took to pursue my dream. I worked hard studying music theory. For songwriting, this came naturally to me. I could only rely on God's grace. Despite all my hard work, I never lost sight of my spiritual purpose. And I stay true to my faith in

God and never let it slip away. I kept my daily devotionals and prayers alive, and they were the first thing I reached for when faced with the obstacles that come with the life of a singer-songwriter.

On creating my first Album, I would read my Bible, trying to understand the concept of biblical analogy. There were times when I would gaze at the skies and reflect on the historical teachings from the Bible that I had learned during the Club hours at church. I would then apply that knowledge to one of the songs I was writing.

Of course, I couldn't solely rely on my strength or ability. I understood the importance of seeking guidance from a higher power. So, I prayed and asked God to lead me and for the Holy Spirit to give me the words to write. This became my method as I continued with the creative process.

Every day, I would spend hours poring over the Scriptures, searching for hidden meanings, and drawing inspiration from the powerful stories within. I sought to weave these timeless truths into my music, hoping to touch the hearts and souls of those who would listen.

As I delved deeper into the Bible, I discovered countless stories and passages that could be reimagined into songs. The story of David's triumph over Goliath resonated with me, reminding me that faith and courage can lead to victory despite seemingly insurmountable obstacles. I channeled these emotions into a song filled with determination and hope.

Another song was born from the story of Noah's Ark. This tale reminded me of the importance of resilience and trust amid adversity. I wanted to capture the essence of Noah and his family's challenges and how their faith ultimately carried them through. This song became an anthem of perseverance and dedication for me.

Each song I wrote allowed me to express my deep reverence for the Scriptures and their messages. I aimed to convey these messages in a way that was both meaningful and accessible. The melodies and lyrics formed a tapestry that brought biblical teachings to life, resonating with listeners profoundly.

The process of creating my first Album was a transformative journey. It allowed me to not only explore my faith but also to share it with others. As I poured my heart and soul into each song, I felt a sense of purpose and fulfillment. The guidance I received from above, along with my dedication and passion, culminated in a collection of music I believed could make a difference.

Looking back, I am grateful for the inspiration I found within the pages of the Bible. My songs became a testament to the power of faith and the impact biblical teachings can have on our lives. I continue to draw from this wisdom and share the beauty of biblical analogy through my music.

As I embarked on my journey to creating my first Album, guided by prayer, reflection, and a deep connection to the Scriptures. Infusing biblical teachings into my songs became a labor of love, resulting in a collection of music that reflected my faith and touched the hearts of others. Through the Holy Spirit's guidance, I found strength, purpose, and inspiration to share the timeless wisdom of the Bible with the world.

I dedicated myself to honing my skills as a singer-songwriter. I spent countless hours practicing, studying music theory, and collaborating with other aspiring artists. The journey was not always easy, but my love for music motivated me to persevere through any obstacles.

***

On the other hand, I acknowledged the depth of responsibility that lay upon my shoulders in creating a remarkable album. I was determined to ensure that every song embodied a Biblical perspective, resonating with the essence of divine teachings. The songs had to transcend mere melodies and be vessels for the profound messages of peace and hope that transcend all boundaries.

Yet, I humbly recognized that I could not embark on this endeavor alone. I yearned for the spiritual guidance and inspiration of the Holy Spirit, for it was through His divine intervention that I would be granted the words to write. Thus, I embarked on a spiritual journey, seeking solace in the tranquility of nature and dedicating hours to prayer and meditation.

One gentle morning, as the sun painted the sky with hues of golden warmth, I ventured into an ancient forest that appeared to whisper secrets of the divine. An overwhelming sense of serenity enveloped me as if the trees were extending their branches in welcome. I closed my eyes, allowing the vibrant symphony of nature to guide my thoughts and grant me clarity.

In this sacred space, my mind became a canvas upon which the Holy Spirit could paint its ethereal masterpiece. Each step I took was infused with a renewed sense of purpose as if guided by an invisible hand that effortlessly steered me towards a path imbued with inspiration.

A gentle breeze caressed my cheeks, carrying echoes of ancient hymns and whispered prayers. As I began to sing, my voice intertwined with the elements around me, echoing through the forest like a musical river. Each song bore testament to the wisdom encoded within Biblical teachings, directing my lyrics towards messages of love, compassion, and unwavering faith.

I poured my heart into each note, daring to expose the deepest corners of my soul in pursuit of lyrical perfection. As if divinely ordained, rhymes danced upon my tongue in perfect harmony with the melodies that emerged from the depths of my being. The notes carried the weight of ancient prophecies and stories, intertwining them seamlessly with contemporary sounds.

Days turned weeks and weeks into months as the album slowly took shape. Each song became a prayer, an offering to a world riddled with despair and longing for solace. With each track, I fervently hoped to kindle a spark of hope in the hearts of those who listened. My mission was to illuminate their darkest nights with the guiding light of faith, to mend their shattered spirits with the suture of divine love.

As the final melodies echoed through the studio, an overwhelming sense of accomplishment washed over me. It was as if the Holy Spirit had lent me wings, carrying me to heights I never dreamed possible. The album, crafted with divine guidance, transcended the boundaries of mere music; it became a testament to the power of faith, a beacon of hope in a world hungering for peace and solace.

Realizing that I could not claim sole credit for this extraordinary creation, I bowed my head in gratitude. Gratitude to the Holy Spirit for His gentle guidance and whispered reassurances throughout this transformative journey. Gratitude to the choir teacher whose collaboration breathed life into these songs, adding vibrant hues to the canvas of faith. Most importantly, I am grateful to those who would soon lend their ears to this melodic testament for imbuing my music with purpose and reminding me of the profound impact hope and peace can have on the human spirit.

As the sun began to set upon the horizon, casting a golden glow upon all that surrounded me, I knew deep within my heart that this album was not solely mine. It belonged to all who craved an escape from the cacophony of everyday life, seeking solace in melodies that carried healing balm for their weary souls. And so, with a newfound sense of purpose, I released this album into the world, praying that it would touch lives, ignite unquenchable flames of faith, and inspire others to embark on their extraordinary journeys of self-discovery and divine connection.

I am filled with gratitude for the path I have traveled. It is a testament to the power of faith, determination, and the unwavering support of loved ones. By believing in myself and relying on God's hand, I fulfilled my dream of becoming a singer. My life is a testimony to the remarkable things that can be accomplished when one follows one's passion and embraces the opportunities that come one way.

In the present time, I continue to create music that speaks to the depths of the human soul, using my voice as an instrument to spread positivity, love, and hope in an ever-changing world. As I look ahead, I am excited to see where this journey will take me next, knowing that with faith as my guide, there is no limit to what I can achieve, most notably, "The Sky's the Limit."

CHAPTER 5

A NEW DIFFERENT WORLD

In 2013, a few months after the debut of my album. The hard work and dedication to creating and releasing it had finally paid off. Its success overjoyed me, but little did I know that an even bigger blessing would come our way.

One fine day, my dad received a letter from the Office of Foreign Affairs. It invited him to the United Nations and represented his country as a diplomat in America. It was a tremendous honor for our family, a once-in-a-lifetime opportunity we couldn't pass up.

My dad had always been a man of integrity and intellect. It was no surprise that his dedication and commitment to his work had earned him this prestigious position. As a diplomat, he would have the chance to interact with world leaders, foster relationships, and represent the interests of his country at the highest international level.

Seeing pride in my father's accomplishments being recognized on such a grand scale was a source of immense satisfaction. As his child, I felt a deep sense of admiration and respect for his achievements. This opportunity meant that our family would have the chance to experience a whole new world rich with diverse cultures and perspectives.

AMID MY QUESTIONABLE EXISTENCE

The summer morning of 2013 was a Sabbath day, right before Sunday. I found myself at the Kigamboni Seventh Day Adventist Church, where my father had to bid farewell to the entire congregation. He had recently secured a job in America and needed to leave our beloved Tanzania behind. As an autobiography, this moment holds a significant place in my memory.

Outside the church, the congregation was gathered, finding shade under the comforting canopies of the surrounding trees. The camaraderie among the members was palpable, yet an air of melancholy pervaded the atmosphere. It was as if everyone instinctively knew that this departure marked the end of an era for our family and the community.

Among the sea of faces, I caught sight of my childhood best friend, Monica. Her eyes brimmed with sorrow, tears rolling down her cheeks, silently reflecting the pain we all felt. Seeing her there, so vulnerable and troubled, tugged at my heartstrings. I approached Monica, wrapping my arms around her to offer solace.

"Don't worry, Monica," I murmured, my voice catching up. "We'll always be friends, no matter the distance."

She clung onto me like a lifeline, finding comfort in our unspoken promise. In that tender moment, I didn't comprehend the lasting impact it would have on our lives. Little did I know that this would be the last time we would meet face to face.

As the months went by, oceans and continents separated us. Our once frequent letters and late-night phone calls grew further apart, succumbing to the demands of time zones and hectic schedules. Life moved on, and so did we.

Years turned into decades, and the memory of that summer morning slowly became a fragment of a distant past. Although we lost touch, our bond remained etched in my heart. The cherished memories we created were a constant reminder of the treasured friendship we once had.

Sadly, life's journey doesn't always allow us to hold onto everything we hold dear. People come and go, and circumstances change. Yet, amid it all, the power of friendship endures.

While Monica and I never had the chance to see each other physically again, the emotional connection we forged as childhood friends remained intact. Our lives took diverging paths, but her impact on me during our time together was immeasurable.

Through various technological advancements, virtual connections bridged the physical distance that separated us. We rekindle our friendship, reminiscing about the carefree days of our childhood and sharing laughter and tears across time zones. The years apart, we seemed to melt away as we rediscovered the essence of our bond.

As I reflect upon that summer morning in 2013, I am reminded of the unpredictable nature of life. The farewell may have marked the end of our physical connection, but it opened the door to a profound appreciation for friendship's intangible values. Monica's tears and our heartfelt embrace symbolized the unbreakable ties that connect souls, transcending time and space.

Ultimately, our friendship endured, defying the limitations of geography and time. The one thing I am sure of is this: no matter where life takes us, the memories we create and the connections we cherish will forever reside within the chambers of our hearts.

Up to our departure, the following day was filled with excitement and anticipation. We started preparing to relocate to the United States, a country known for its diverse landscapes, iconic landmarks, and unparalleled opportunities.

The summer of 2013 brought about a significant turning point in our lives. The invitation for my dad to represent his country at the United Nations in America was a blessing that opened doors to new opportunities and expanded our horizons. It was a moment of pride and joy for our family and an experience I will forever hold dear.

Upon our arrival to the United States, my dad and I. Mr. Swele welcomed us at the John F. Kennedy International Airport. Back in Tanzania, my mom remained, patiently waiting for my big sister to finish her high school diploma before joining us the following year, in 2014.

We arrived at Roosevelt Island, an island located in the heart of the bustling city of New York, and there was a small island known as Roosevelt Island. This peculiar place had a charm, with its rich history and unique character.

It was said that the island was named after President Franklin D. Roosevelt, who had left an indelible mark on the nation.

Legend had it that Roosevelt Island was once a haven for outcasts and misfits. In the early 19th century, it was home to a lunatic asylum, where those deemed "insane" were sent to live out their days. The island symbolized isolation and despair, but little did the world know it would soon transform into something extraordinary.

The asylum was closed as time passed, and the island underwent a remarkable metamorphosis. It became a vibrant community, attracting people from all walks of life. The island's main attraction was the iconic tramway, a suspended cable car that connected Roosevelt

Island to Manhattan. It was a thrilling ride, offering breathtaking views of the city skyline.

The island was also known for its peaceful parks and gardens, providing a serene escape from the chaos of the city. Visitors could stroll along the promenade, admiring the East River as it flowed gracefully. The island's lighthouse, a beacon of hope, stood tall and proud, guiding ships safely through the treacherous waters.

One of the island's most fascinating features was the Smallpox Hospital, a hauntingly beautiful ruin that reminded of the island's dark past. It was a place where history whispered through the crumbling walls, telling tales of the patients who once sought solace within its halls.

But perhaps the most enchanting aspect of Roosevelt Island was its sense of community. The residents were a tight-knit group, always ready to lend a helping hand or share a friendly smile. They organized events and festivals, celebrating the island's diversity and unity.

The island hosts a grand celebration called Roosevelt Island Day every year. The streets would come alive with music, laughter, and the mouthwatering aroma of street food. People from all over the city flocked to the island, eager to experience the magic that Roosevelt Island had to offer.

As the sun set over the city, casting a golden glow upon the island, the residents gathered at the waterfront for a mesmerizing fireworks display. The sky exploded with vibrant colors, reflecting off the shimmering waters below. It was a moment of pure joy and wonder, a testament to the island's resilience and spirit.

And so, Roosevelt Island continued to thrive, a hidden gem in the heart of New York City. Its rich history, breathtaking views, and vibrant community made it a place like no other. As the years passed, the island's story unfolded, captivating the hearts and minds of all who ventured there.

This is where our family would be residing for the next four years. The Swele family, with Mr. Swele as our host, warmly welcomed us. He introduced us to his family, including his daughters, Rose and Catherine. Mr. Swele informed us that one of his older children had tragically passed away, and his wife was currently in Tanzania.

***

The day after, my dad and my young sibling arrived at Roosevelt; it was a bright and sunny day when we had just started settling into a place where we would be living for the next four years before the Swele family transitioned to Washington D.C. We were eager to explore our new surroundings. Little did we know that an extraordinary encounter awaited us the very next day.

As morning turned to afternoon, two tiny figures approached our front door. I could hear the faint sound of knocking and hurriedly made my way to answer it. To my surprise, two young children, accompanied by their mother, wore smiles that radiated joy and love.

The little girl, Joycelyn, and her brother, Jonathan, were delighted. They enthusiastically rode their scooters, their faces gleaming excitedly as they entered our home. They were adorable, and I couldn't help but be captivated by their innocence and charm.

There was something unique about this family that immediately drew me in. It was their positive and friendly demeanor that fostered an instant connection. The warmth in their eyes and the kindness in their words made me feel welcomed and accepted as if I had known them for a lifetime.

In the following days, I spent more time getting to know Joycelyn, Jonathan, and their mother. We shared stories and laughter, creating memories forever etched in my heart. Their vibrant spirits and unwavering support became integral to my life as our families grew closer each day.

Through the years, we faced various challenges together, and their unwavering encouragement and strength propelled us forward. Joycelyn and Jonathan became more than just friends; they became siblings I never had. And their mother, a pillar of wisdom and understanding, became a guiding light in my journey.

Reflecting upon these cherished memories, I am grateful for the encounter that brought us together. Their impact on my life is immeasurable, and I attribute my growth and success to their love and support.

Above all, my story would only be complete with mentioning Joycelyn, Jonathan, and their mother. They taught me the value of friendship, the power of positivity, and the importance of family. Their presence in my life has forever shaped me into the person I am today, and for that, I will be eternally thankful.

There was something unique about this family that immediately drew me in. It was their positive and friendly demeanor that fostered an instant connection. The warmth in their eyes and kindness in their words made me feel welcomed and accepted, as if I had known them for a lifetime.

Later, we quickly developed a close bond with the Swele family. Being close to us, Ms. Rose became an older sister, while Catherine became our little sister. Together, we shared laughter, played games, and embarked on exciting adventures throughout the vibrant city of New York.

Exploring the city became a highlight of our time on Roosevelt Island. With Mr. Swele's guidance and our newfound siblings' enthusiasm, we ventured to various places, discovering new sights and experiences. The bustling streets, iconic landmarks, and diverse neighborhoods of New York City never failed to enthrall us.

We visited renowned museums, such as the Metropolitan Museum of Art and the American Museum of Natural History, immersing ourselves in the rich cultural and historical treasures they offered. The vibrant energy of Times Square and the magnificent skyline of Manhattan left us in awe.

Central Park became a cherished sanctuary amidst the metropolitan chaos. We spent countless afternoons strolling through its winding paths, taking in the beauty of nature and indulging in delightful picnics. The park's tranquil atmosphere provided solace amid the bustling city.

Our exploration extended beyond the city's boundaries as well. We took memorable trips to nearby attractions, such as the Statue of Liberty, Ellis Island, and the awe-inspiring Niagara Falls. Each new destination brought a sense of wonder and appreciation for the vastness and diversity of our surroundings.

As the years passed, our time on Roosevelt Island became etched as moments of marvel and excitement. Our experiences with the Swele family shaped our lives and broadened our horizons. We developed a deeper understanding of different cultures, nurtured lifelong friendships, and learned to appreciate the beauty of both the concrete jungle and the green oases within.

The transition from Roosevelt Island to Washington D.C. marked the end of our chapter with the Swele family. However, the bond we formed with them and the memories we created will forever hold a special place in our hearts. The years spent on Roosevelt Island were pivotal in our lives, where we discovered the joys of exploration, the importance of community, and the power of friendship.

At the same time, I stood alongside my second sister, Rosie, at Roosevelt. She introduced us to the Adventist church known as Bayanihan SDA Church. Nestled in Long Island, in the borough of Queens, this church became a warm and cozy sanctuary for us. I had the incredible opportunity to forge heartfelt connections with every church family member. Looking back, I am sincerely grateful for this community's deep sense of belonging.

I extend my wholehearted appreciation to everyone who became integral to my church family. Everyone made a lasting impact on my life, shaping me into the person I am today. Their unwavering support and genuine care were a constant source of inspiration.

One person whom I distinctly remember is Pastor Wong. He had a remarkable ability to connect with people on a personal level. I would often find solace in his comforting presence and compassionate words. Pastor Wong's dedication to his role as a spiritual leader was evident in his commitment to the well-being of the church members.

There were countless memorable moments spent within the walls of Bayanihan SDA Church. The church program was always a highlight, with its uplifting music and inspiring sermons. We would gather as a united congregation, sharing the joy of worship and fellowship. As the program ended, Pastor Wong graciously offered my family and me a ride home if it was too late. His kindness and concern for my well-being stood as a testament to the extraordinary unity within the church.

A sense of phenomenology characterized every experience at Bayanihan SDA Church. The genuine friendships, the deep-rooted faith, and the unwavering support from the church family made every moment special. It felt like a second home, filled with love, acceptance, and spiritual growth.

Reflecting upon my time at Bayanihan Seventh Day Adventist Church (Filipino) fills me with gratitude and nostalgia. The warmth and coziness of the church, the bonds formed within the community, and the unwavering support will always hold a cherished place in my heart.

Through these experiences, I truly understood the power of a close-knit church family.

I am forever grateful to have been part of such a remarkable community. Bayanihan SDA Church was not just a place of worship but a sanctuary where lifelong friendships were forged and where I grew in my faith. Each memory I have from my time there is a testament to the extraordinary love and unity that permeated every aspect of church life. As I continue my journey, I carry the lessons learned, the bonds formed, and the unwavering support of the Bayanihan SDA Church family deep within my being.

Reflecting upon our time in New York City, we were grateful for the opportunity to call Roosevelt Island our home. It was a privilege to be part of the Swele family's lives, and their warm hospitality left an indelible imprint on our lives before they left for Washington, D.C.

Mr. Swele, our kind host, provided valuable information about the American education system. He highlighted the importance of finding a school that would suit my needs and aspirations. He encouraged us to consider a school that valued diversity and provided excellent academic programs with the help of the Mkapa family.

Armed with this guidance, my dad and I began to find the perfect educational institution. We researched extensively, seeking schools with a solid academic excellence reputation and a welcoming atmosphere for international students.

Our search led us to visit several schools in the area. I vividly remember the crisp fall mornings we spent visiting campuses, meeting staff members, and attending presentations. It was an exciting time filled with anticipation and nervousness.

We stayed for the rest of the summer break, searching for the right school for me to attend before the fall semester began. As new immigrants, we were determined to find a place where I could pursue my education and thrive in the land of opportunities.

> Living on Roosevelt Island, we embraced the opportunities to engage with the community. We participated in local events, volunteered at nearby shelters, and developed lasting friendships with our neighbors. The sense of belonging

and interconnectedness within the community was truly heartwarming.

Finally, after carefully weighing our options, we found a school that resonated with my goals and values. It was a prestigious institution known for its commitment to fostering a diverse community and providing a well-rounded education. The campus exuded an aura of knowledge and growth, making it the ideal environment for my educational journey.

Enrolling in the school was just the beginning. Adjusting to the American education system, culture, and lifestyle proved challenging. However, I was determined to make the most of this opportunity and excel in my studies.

The day finally came for me and my little sister. We started on our school journey. My little sister attended middle school at Roosevelt Island, while I attended Manhattan International High School in the Manhattan borough. For transportation, I used to commute by F train or the Tram. Interestingly, some students and teachers went to Manhattan International High School. Every morning, we would see each other on the Tram or Subway and walk together afterward.

The transition brought about a whirlwind of experiences. From navigating a new curriculum to learning the intricacies of American social norms, I constantly adapted and embraced the diversity surrounding me. I made friends from different cultural backgrounds and engaged in stimulating discussions that broadened my perspectives.

The school provided me with numerous growth opportunities. I immersed myself in extracurricular activities, joining clubs and participating in community service projects. These experiences helped me develop leadership skills and created lasting friendships and memories.

As the child of a diplomat, my experiences were unique. I had the privilege of attending an international school, where I met classmates worldwide. We shared stories and ideas and formed lifelong friendships. The exposure to different cultures broadened my horizons and expanded my understanding of the world.

On my first day of classes at Manhattan International High School, located at 317 East

67th Street, I was warmly welcomed by one of the school secretaries. Unfortunately, I can't recall precisely who escorted me to class, but I believe it was Ms. Daira Olivero, Ms. Wioleta Metel, or Ms. Bogumila Snihur. The secretary guided me to my first class, which Ms. Gallia Kassiano taught in 9th grade.

I was taken aback when I saw Ms. Kassiano. I initially mistook her for one of the students due to her youthful appearance. However, to my surprise, one of the secretaries informed me that she would be my homeroom teacher for the entire school year.

As I entered the classroom, I noticed diverse students from various backgrounds. It was indeed a melting pot of cultures and experiences. This mixture of personalities and perspectives fascinated me, and I eagerly looked forward to getting to know every one of my classmates.

Throughout the year, Ms. Kassiano proved to be an exceptional teacher. Her dedication to her students was evident in her well-prepared lessons and engaging teaching style. She seamlessly blended traditional teaching methods with modern, interactive techniques, making every class a stimulating experience.

Ms. Kassiano's class taught us academic subjects and valuable life skills. She encouraged us to think critically, question assumptions, and express ourselves confidently. Her ability to create a safe and inclusive environment allowed us to share our thoughts and ideas without fear of judgment freely.

Under her guidance, I witnessed the transformation of an ordinary classroom into a vibrant community of learners. Students who were initially shy and reserved gradually opened up, showcasing their unique talents and contributing to class discussions. Ms. Kassiano fostered an atmosphere where everyone's voice was heard, fostering a sense of belonging and unity.

Looking back, I realize that my time in Ms. Kassiano's class was not just about acquiring knowledge but about personal growth. She instilled in us the importance of perseverance, empathy, and respect. These invaluable life lessons continue to shape the person I am today.

As the school year ended, I couldn't help but feel a sense of gratitude towards Ms. Kassiano and my diverse group of classmates. We journeyed together through challenges and triumphs, forming lasting friendships and transcending cultural boundaries.

My experience was in Ms. Kassiano's class, Mr. Moses Ahn, who taught global history, and Ms. Nelly Choueiri, who taught Mathematics. Ms. Marie, who taught Chemistry, and Mr. Rick, who taught PE. Both teachers taught me that education is not just about grades and exams. It's about fostering a passion for learning, embracing diversity, and equipping oneself with the tools to navigate the ever-changing world.

I remember the day when I had just gotten off the global history class taught by Mr. Moses; as I left the classroom, I saw one of the students also in my class, Patience. We introduced ourselves and where we were coming from. We didn't know each other as new students who just started their high school journey.

Rachel: Hi there! I noticed we're in the same Global History class. I'm Rachel, by the way.

Patience: Oh, hello, Rachel! Nice to meet you. I'm Patience. Are you new here, too?

Rachel: Yes, I am! I just started my high school journey. How about you?

Patience: Same here! This is my first year, too. I was a bit nervous, but now I'm starting to settle in. Where are you from?

Rachel: I'm from Tanzania. What about you?

Patience: Oh, that's interesting! I'm from Ghana. We both have African roots!

Rachel: That's amazing! I've always been curious about life in other African countries. What brought you here?

Patience: My family moved here for better opportunities and education. I'm excited to experience a different culture and meet new people. How about you?

Rachel: Similar reasons! My parents thought it would be an excellent chance for me to explore new horizons and gain a broader perspective on global history. It's been an adventure so far.

Patience: I agree. It's sometimes a bit overwhelming, but we'll adjust just fine. Have you met many other students in our class?

Rachel: Not really. I've only spoken to a few students, but making new friends is always great. It's nice to have someone to navigate this journey with.

Patience: Absolutely! We should stick together. A familiar face can make all the difference. Plus, we can support each other through the highs and lows of high school life.

Rachel: I couldn't agree more. Meeting someone who understands the excitement and challenges of being new to this environment is refreshing. Let's make the most out of this journey together, Patience!

Patience: Definitely, Rachel! I look forward to getting to know you better and making this high school experience memorable. Thank you for reaching out!

Rachel: It's my pleasure, Patience. We're going to have a fantastic time here. Let's make the most of our classes and take every opportunity that comes our way!

Patience: Absolutely! Nice to meet you, fellow African!

I will forever cherish the memories and lessons learned in that 9th-grade classroom, and I am grateful for the profound impact Ms. Kassiano and the rest of the teachers had on my life. They shaped me as a student and an individual, preparing me to face the world with confidence, empathy, and an insatiable thirst for knowledge.

It was a great moment that brought us together, Patience, and a group of classmates at Manhattan International High School. We were all 9th graders, embarking on a new year of studying.

It was a thrilling experience getting to know Patience and the others. The air was filled with excitement and anticipation as they gathered to share stories and learn about each other. The atmosphere was buzzing with the energy of new friendships forming.

As the days went by, Patience and I grew closer. We discovered and shared our interests and aspirations. We supported each other through the challenges of schoolwork and celebrated successes together. It was a bond that would last a lifetime.

The journey of friendship and learning continued throughout the year. Patience and I, together with another group of classmates, became a tight-knit community, always there for each other. As we navigated the halls of Manhattan International High School together, facing the ups and downs of high school life.

Ultimately, it was about more than just the academic achievements or the grades we received. It was about the memories we created, the lessons we learned, and the friendships that blossomed. My classmates and I became a family united by their shared experiences and our love for each other.

And so, the great moment of getting to know Patience and her classmates became a cherished memory. It was a reminder of the power of friendship and the beauty of connections made in unexpected places. As we moved on to higher grades and different paths in life, we would always carry the special bond we formed in our hearts.

Living abroad also taught me about resilience and adaptability. Being in an unfamiliar environment and constantly adjusting to new customs and traditions was sometimes challenging. However, these challenges only made me stronger and more open-minded.

****

Throughout our time in America, my dad continued to excel as a diplomat. He effectively represented his country's interests and worked tirelessly to build bridges between nations. Witnessing his dedication and diplomacy firsthand was both inspiring and humbling.

Growing up, my father was the sole parent responsible for caring for my younger sister and me. As we attended school, our lives were a whirlwind of balancing academics and household responsibilities. One evening stands out vividly - when my sister and I attempted to cook a meal for our hardworking father.

It began like any ordinary day. The sun illuminated the sky, casting golden hues upon our small, cozy home. My sister and I had just returned from school, tired yet eager to unwind in the comforting presence of our doting father. As we stepped through the threshold, the familiar aroma of warm meals enveloped us, flooding our senses with delightful anticipation.

Our dad, a remarkable figure of unconditional love and affection, would always have a delicious dinner ready for us. His culinary skills were second to none, and we relished the meals he painstakingly crafted with love. But on that day, something was different. A peculiar feeling seized my sister and me, tugging at our hearts as if urging us to reciprocate our father's affection extraordinarily.

Inspired by this newfound determination, we exchanged knowing glances and wordlessly agreed to embark on a special mission for our beloved father. Together, we ventured into our domain of flavors and spices—the kitchen—a place previously reserved for our father's watchful eyes and nimble hands alone. But armed with enthusiasm and a sense of responsibility, we ventured forward, eager to demonstrate our devotion through culinary delights.

As we stood side by side in front of the stove, its flickering flames danced before our eyes, captivating and intimidating. The furnace seemed like an unfamiliar monster, a formidable challenge that dared us to conquer. Yet, undeterred by its fiery presence, we summoned courage and pressed onward.

Our culinary adventure commenced by scouring the pantry for ingredients. With limited knowledge of cooking and only our instincts as guides, we explored the shelves, letting our fingers dance across glass jars and boxes. Together, we selected various spices, from humble salt and pepper to exotic blends that whispered tales of distant lands.

In our youthful exuberance, my little sister and I meticulously chopped vibrant vegetables, their colors reminiscent of a painter's palette. The tantalizing aroma of herbs wafted through the air, transforming our humble kitchen into a fragrant sanctuary. Like alchemists, we mixed spices, sprinkling vibrant specks of flavor into the simmering pot. The concoction came alive with each stir, promising an exceptional meal.

As we toiled away, time seemed to stand still. Our imaginations ran wild, envisioning our father's surprised expression when he discovered the feast we had prepared for him. A smile etched itself upon our faces, a testament to the burgeoning pride swelling within our hearts. Though the stove remained a formidable adversary, we refused to surrender, determined to conquer it and present a meal worthy of our father's unconditional love and care.

The aroma grew even more enticing as the final touches were made, teasing our senses and luring our father towards the dining table. We stood side by side, anticipation mingling with apprehension. The clock ticked with measured excitement as we awaited his arrival.

Then, the moment arrived. Our father stepped through the door, his eyes widening in surprise as the tantalizing scent guided him toward the feast that awaited him. A surge of satisfaction surged as he loomed over the dishes we had crafted with love and care.

Time, he stood still as our father took his first bite. His face lit up with joy, a radiant smile illuminating his features. At that moment, we knew we had succeeded. Our culinary experiment delighted his taste buds and profoundly touched his heart.

The dinner became a symphony of laughter and appreciation, an evening etched into our shared memories. As we savored each bite and soaked up the warmth of familial love, my sister and I basked in a sense of accomplishment—not just because we had conquered the unfamiliar monster of the stove but because our actions had touched our father's heart.

In the years to come, our culinary journeys would evolve, guided by experience and further knowledge. But the memory of that ordinary day turned extraordinary would forever hold a special place in our hearts—a reminder of the magic that unfolds when love, determination, and a touch of youthful innocence converge in the kitchen.

***

Moving forward to one of my memorable encounters while living in Roosevelt Island after a few months of moving in, my family and I had an excellent opportunity to meet our fellow family members from Tanzania, including the Mkapa family, the Kisota family, the Manongi family, the Mero family, and the rest of the families. I am so grateful to have formed a short bond with the families.

While living in Roosevelt Island, after a few months of moving in, my family and I had an excellent opportunity to meet our fellow family members from Tanzania. It was an incredible experience to connect with people from different cultures and backgrounds.

Among the families we met were the Mkapa family, the Kisota family, the Manongi family, the Mero family, and many others. Each family had a unique story, and learning about their traditions, values, and way of life was fascinating.

I am so grateful to have had the chance to form a short but meaningful bond with these families. We shared meals, exchanged stories, and created memories that will last a lifetime. It was a beautiful reminder of the power of human connection and the joy of embracing diversity.

As the days passed, we realized we were all connected by our shared humanity despite our differences. Our conversations were filled with laughter, curiosity, and a genuine desire to understand and appreciate each other's perspectives.

The experience taught me the importance of embracing diversity and celebrating our world's rich tapestry of cultures. It reminded me that there is so much we can learn from one another if we open our hearts and minds.

Even though our time together was short, the impact of those interactions will stay with me forever. The friendships we formed transcended borders and reminded us that love and kindness know no boundaries.

I will forever cherish the memories spent with the families from Tanzania. It was a truly transformative experience that taught me the power of connection, empathy, and the beauty of embracing different cultures.

The experiences determining the gentle bond fostered that night continue to be one of my most remarkable memories from childhood. Seeing so many families from faraway countries uniting to celebrate family ties certainly brightened my days for years to come.

I also had many unique experiences while living on Roosevelt Island, including the parks, with their side river view stretching from right to left or left to right. The people living there were early risers, and they left a lasting impression on me.

The sounds of children playing around the park or on the playground filled the air, creating a magical atmosphere. It was as if the laughter and joy of the little ones were contagious, spreading happiness to everyone around.

What made this time even more special was the opportunity my family and I had to meet people from different backgrounds. We encountered individuals from Asia, the Middle East, and Europe, each bringing their unique cultures and traditions to the community.

In this diverse melting pot, we formed an incredible bond of friendship. We shared stories, exchanged cultural experiences, and celebrated our differences. It was a beautiful tapestry of human connection where unity and understanding thrived.

Living on Roosevelt Island taught me the value of embracing diversity and opening my heart to new experiences. It was a chapter of my life that I will always cherish, for it showed me the beauty of a community coming together, celebrating life, and creating lasting memories.

****

In the heart of Roosevelt Island, nestled amidst the hustle and bustle of city life, my family and I embarked on a brand-new chapter. Leaving behind the breathtaking landscapes of Tanzania, we found ourselves in this vibrant neighborhood, eager to forge connections with fellow Tanzanian families who called this place home.

As we settled into our new abode, the air was filled with excitement and anticipation. Our hearts yearned for familiarity, friendship, and the comforting presence of our native culture. Little did we know that destiny held something special for us in the form of the Kisota family.

The Kisotas were not just neighbors; they were a ray of sunshine brightly radiating from their humble abode. With hearts full of warmth and spirits brimming with infectious energy, they embraced life with open arms and made every moment count. Their laughter echoed through the hallways, their joy weaving an enchanting tapestry that drew us in like a magnet.

Jonathan and Jocelyn, the enthusiastic children of the Kisota family, were kindred spirits to us. Like kindred souls intertwining in a dance of friendship, my little sister and I found solace in their company. Every weekend, as the sun painted vivid strokes across the horizon, our feet would carry us toward their doorstep. Oh, what delightful adventures awaited us behind those welcoming walls!

From dawn till dusk, we would lose ourselves in a symphony of childhood innocence. Imagination soared as we fashioned castles from blankets and sailed imaginary seas upon cushions. Our laughter chimed like bells in the wind as we concocted make-believe tales transcending time and space.

And oh, those summer vacations! With schoolbooks set aside and freedom embraced, our days melted seamlessly into one another at the Kisota household. From savoring indulgent breakfasts on golden mornings to bidding farewell to twilight's embrace, our lives danced to the rhythm of vibrant camaraderie and carefree bliss.

AMID MY QUESTIONABLE EXISTENCE

The Kisota family's house became our sanctuary, a haven where cultural boundaries blurred and traditions from distant lands intertwined harmoniously with the city's beats. Amidst mouthwatering aromas wafting from their kitchen, we would embark on culinary expeditions, blending Tanzanian delicacies with local flavors. The tantalizing scents enveloped us like a warm embrace, comforting our souls and reminding us of the home we had temporarily left behind.

Time would stand still within those walls, and before we knew it, the sun would bid farewell, casting long shadows over the horizon. But even as twilight arrived, the laughter never ceased, and the bond between our families only grew stronger. Safe in the embrace of cherished friendships, we revealed the beauty of shared memories that painted vivid strokes upon the canvases of our hearts.

As we returned home, our spirits aglow with a sense of belonging. We couldn't help but marvel at the serendipitous path that had led us to Roosevelt Island. In the vast tapestry of life, we had discovered a second family – the Kisota family – who had woven themselves into our lives with threads of love and laughter.

And so, in that little neighborhood oasis where cultures converged and friendships blossomed, the walls hummed with stories waiting to be told, our hearts found solace. In the spirit of Roosevelt Island, a new chapter unfolded, filled with the magic that can only be found when souls from distant lands collide and create a melody that dances upon the winds of time.

***

In the year before my mom and sister officially became part of our family, my dad embarked on a short business trip to Tanzania. This left me alone with my little sister, Mbuke. Though we were apprehensive about being without our parents, we were fortunate to have the Mkapa family step in to care for us during this time.

Sister Fatuma, a warm-hearted woman with a comforting presence, volunteered to come and spend the nights at our house. She knew how to ease our worries and make us feel safe and loved, just like our parents would. Her presence made the days seem less long and the nights less lonely.

In addition to taking care of our emotional well-being, Aunt Mkapa, whom I affectionately called Shangazi in Swahili, was responsible for ensuring that my medical needs were met. She would accompany me to the prestigious New York-Presbyterian/Weill Cornell Medical Center for regular check-ups.

I vividly remember one visit when we went to have my ears checked. I had been experiencing pain and difficulty hearing due to fluid build-up. The kind doctors at the medical center performed a minor procedure to remove the fluid, alleviating my discomfort and improving my hearing. With Aunt Mkapa by my side, I felt brave and supported.

After we left the hospital, Aunt Mkapa took me back home. Her nurturing presence made me feel safe even in unfamiliar circumstances. Little did I know that Aunt Mkapa's care and compassion extended beyond just me; she also looked after my older sister, Happen when she underwent surgery to remove her wisdom teeth the following year.

It was a challenging time for Happen, as she needed to recover from her surgery without our parents by her side. However, Aunt Mkapa's kindness knew no bounds. She dedicated herself to ensuring that she felt comforted and cared for during her healing process. Aunt Mkapa's gentle words, warm soups, and soothing stories helped Happen to recover quickly and happily.

Those days of temporary separation from our parents were made more accessible and filled with love, thanks to the benevolence and support of Aunt Mkapa and her family. Their willingness to step in and treat us as their own was a gift.

As the years went on and our family bonds grew more substantial, we never forgot the incredible kindness shown to us during that time. It reminded us that compassion knows no boundaries and that good-hearted individuals are always ready to lend a helping hand.

We are forever grateful to Aunt Mkapa, Sister Fatuma, and all those who helped and nurtured us when our parents were away. Your acts of love have left an indelible mark on our hearts, constantly reminding us of the beauty that lies within humanity.

In 2015, after a period of separation, my mother and sister finally joined us in the United States during the summer. It was a moment filled with joy and relief as we reunited as a family. To me, it was a special occasion that I will forever cherish.

The journey to bring my mother and sister to the United States was long and arduous. We had been apart for years, and the distance between us sometimes seemed impossible. However, perseverance and determination overcame the obstacles and made our dream of being together a reality.

When the day finally arrived, my heart was filled with anticipation. My dad went to the airport to pick them up as he stood at the airport gate, watching the passengers disembark the plane. His eyes searched eagerly for the familiar faces of our loved ones. And there they were, walking towards me with smiles and tears of joy in their eyes.

The reunion was nothing short of magical. We embraced each other tightly as if to compensate for the lost time. The years apart had been difficult, but all the pain and longing melted away in that moment. We were together again, and that's all that mattered.

From that day forward, we formed a robust support system for each other. We celebrated each milestone, big or small, cheering each other on as we pursued our goals. My sister excelled in her studies, my mother found a fulfilling job, and I continued to work towards my dreams. We were each other's biggest fans, pushing each other to reach our full potential.

Family gatherings became something we treasured. Whether it was a birthday celebration, a holiday gathering, or a simple dinner at home, we cherished every moment spent together. The laughter, the conversations, and the shared experiences brought us closer as a family.

As the years went by, our bond only grew stronger. We faced challenges and setbacks, but we met them together. Our love and support for one another gave us the strength to overcome any obstacle that came our way.

Looking back, I realize how fortunate I am to have my family by my side. The joy I felt when we were finally reunited in 2014 remains one of the most special memories of my life. We may have come from different places and faced other struggles, but we created a story of resilience, love, and triumph.

In the end, it is the love of family that sustains us through life's ups and downs. Reflecting on our journey, I am grateful for the unwavering support and love my mother and sister gave me. They have been my pillars of strength, and I know that if we have each other, we can overcome anything.

As the years go on, I treasure the moments we share and hold onto the memories we've created. The reunion of our family in 2014 marked the beginning of a new chapter in our lives, one filled with love, support, and endless possibilities. And I am grateful daily for the blessings of having my mother and sister by my side.

In 2014, we brought my long-awaited reunion with my mother and sister in the United States. Together, we formed a robust support system and celebrated each milestone. The joy of seeing our family together again remains one of my most special memories.

Reflecting upon my journey, I am grateful for the opportunity to have studied in the United States. The education I received and the experiences I gained have shaped me into the person I am today. The resilience, adaptability, and cultural understanding I developed while in America continue to guide my path as I pursue my dreams.

AMID MY QUESTIONABLE EXISTENCE

Leaving my homeland and starting anew in a foreign land was undoubtedly challenging. However, with unwavering determination and the support of my family, I overcame obstacles and transformed them into stepping stones towards a brighter future.

As a young immigrant pursuing education and growth, I am capturing the essence of resilience, determination, and gratitude. It reflects the United States' countless opportunities and the unwavering support and love of a family united by pursuing a better life.

In 2014, sister Rosie introduced my family and me to the Filipino church at Bayanihan Seventh Day Adventist Church. My mom and sister have already arrived in the United

States. In the summer of 2014, my sister and I were involved in the Pathfinder Club at Bayanihan SDA Church with our mom. Little did we know that this experience would shape our lives in ways we could never have imagined.

One memory stands out among the rest - our unforgettable trip to Oshkosh. Oshkosh is an international camporee held every five years where around 50,000 Pathfinders from nearly 100 countries gather to play, share, learn, and worship together. This event provided a unique opportunity for young people to strengthen their relationship with God and create lasting bonds with fellow Pathfinders.

My little sister and I were new to obtaining the Pathfinder uniform. Brother Andy, a church youth program director, arranged it for us. The uniform consisted of a black skirt, a light brown shirt, a black hat with the Pathfinder logo, and other pieces. The process was marvelous, and I am grateful to have gone through it.

Stepping onto the campgrounds, we were awe-struck by the sheer magnitude of the event. Tents and flags representing different countries filled the landscape, creating a vibrant tapestry of cultures. The atmosphere was charged with energy and excitement as Pathfinders from all corners of the globe converged in one place.

The days were filled with a plethora of activities and workshops. From hiking to crafts to survival skills, there was something for everyone. We eagerly participated in various seminars, soaking up knowledge and skills that would prove invaluable on our journey through life.

These activities taught us practical skills and fostered a sense of camaraderie and teamwork among our fellow Pathfinders.

I was excited about meeting the Loma Linda Pathfinder Club! There were so many members that I couldn't even count them. They are one of my favorite Pathfinder Clubs at Camporee, and I couldn't wait to meet them in person! WOW!

Friendships were formed amidst the hustle and bustle of the camporee. We met Pathfinders from different countries with unique stories and backgrounds. Our shared faith and everyday experiences provided a strong foundation for lasting connections despite the language barriers. These newfound friendships became integral to our lives, transcending borders and bringing together young people worldwide.

Amidst the various activities, worship played a central role in our time at Oshkosh. Gathered under a vast sky, we lifted our voices in praise and worship, immersing ourselves in the spiritual experience. It was a powerful reminder of the global community of believers we belonged to. The bond we formed with God and each other during these moments of worship was unparalleled.

As the camporee ended, we couldn't help but feel a deep sense of gratitude for this once-in-a-lifetime opportunity. The memories we made and the lessons we learned at Oshkosh will forever be etched in our hearts. It was a transformative experience that strengthened our faith, broadened our horizons, and shaped us into the individuals we are today.

The Pathfinder Club at Bayanihan SDA Church taught us the power of community, the importance of faith, and the beauty of embracing diversity. Through our involvement, we built a strong connection with each other as young people and expanded our global network of friends. Our journey to Oshkosh was a testament to the incredible experiences that await those who seek to grow in their faith and explore the world.

Looking back, Oshkosh remains the most significant memory of my life. It was a chapter of self-discovery, adventure, and spiritual growth that will forever hold a special place in my heart. The Pathfinder Club and its opportunities opened doors to a world of possibilities, instilling values that continue to guide us on our lifelong journey with God.

One of the most cherished memories from my time as a Bayanihan Seventh Day Adventist Church member was my involvement in the Pathfinder Club. Accompanied by my little sister and her friend Crystal, we embarked on a journey of discovery and growth. The Pathfinder Club provided us with an opportunity to deepen our understanding of God's creation and an avenue for engaging in various activities.

Our involvement in the Pathfinder Club was filled with joyous experiences I will forever hold dear. One notable aspect was the numerous camps we had the privilege of attending. The Greater New York Pathfinder Camporee and the base held at Camp Berkshires were among the most memorable.

Attending the Greater New York Pathfinder Camporee was an enriching experience. We had the opportunity to engage with fellow Pathfinders from various churches, fostering a sense of unity and camaraderie. The camporee offered many activities that tested our skills and capabilities, instilling a sense of perseverance and determination. From team-building exercises to outdoor adventures, each moment was precious to me.

Camp Berkshires was another significant camp that left an indelible mark on my life. Surrounded by nature's beauty, we immersed ourselves in its tranquil embrace. The center provided the perfect backdrop for us to delve into the intricate wonders of God's creation. Through interactive workshops, we learned about the diverse flora and fauna that inhabit our world, deepening our appreciation for the complex balance of nature.

In addition to these memorable camps, the Pathfinder Club also organized various other activities that allowed us to express our talents. From music lessons to community service initiatives, we learned the importance of utilizing our abilities to improve society. Through these experiences, I discovered the joy of serving others, fostering a sense of purpose and fulfillment.

My involvement in the Pathfinder Club, my little sister, and our friend Crystal forged bonds that transcend time. Together, we navigated the path toward spiritual growth, embracing the teachings of our faith while cherishing the company of like-minded individuals.

Looking back on those formative years, I am grateful for the opportunities the Pathfinder Club provided me. The memories formed during those times testify to the power of community, faith, and self-discovery. The experiences at the Greater New York Pathfinder Camporee and Camp Berkshires will forever remain etched in my mind as a reminder of the transformative potential within each of us.

As I reflect upon my life, I am reminded of the incredible privilege I had to be a part of the Pathfinder Club. With humility and gratitude, I acknowledge its profound impact on shaping my character and fostering a lifelong commitment to faith, community, and service.

I embarked on a new journey as I continued my High School year in 2015. Full of hopes and dreams, I was about to transition to 10th grade at Manhattan International High School.

As the summer ended, I felt excitement and nervousness for the new beginning. I had heard great things about my school and couldn't wait to start this new chapter of my academic life—the thought of meeting new friends and experiencing new opportunities filled my mind with anticipation.

The first day of school arrived, and I woke up with butterflies. I wore my best outfit, packed my bag with all the necessary supplies, and headed out the door. Walking through the school doo, I couldn't help but feel a sense of awe at the grandeur of the building.

I tried connecting with my classmates in the first few weeks of 10th grade. I introduced myself and participated in group projects. Slowly but surely, I began to form friendships that would last a lifetime. Together, we navigated the ups and downs of high school life, supporting each other along the way.

As the school year progressed, I faced various academic challenges. The workload became more demanding, and I had to adapt to new subjects and teaching styles. However, with determination and the support of my teachers and friends, I overcame these obstacles and grew both academically and personally.

AMID MY QUESTIONABLE EXISTENCE

As a student, I discovered my true passions within the walls of Manhattan International High School. I found joy and fulfillment in pursuing my interests through art, science, and literature. I joined extracurricular activities related to my passions, honed my skills, and even won awards for my achievements.

As the year ended, I couldn't help but reflect on my journey. I had grown so much since that first day of 10th grade. The friendships, the challenges, and the passions they discovered had shaped them into a more confident and resilient individual. With my eyes set on the future, I felt ready to take on whatever came their way.

And so, my transition to 10th grade at Manhattan International High School became a pivotal moment in their life. It was a year of growth, learning, and self-discovery. As we closed this chapter, I knew the memories and lessons learned would forever be cherished.

While continuing my studies at Manhattan International High School, a persistent feeling in my heart urged me to pursue singing. However, I needed clarification on how and where to begin. In those moments, I dismissed this innate calling and instead remained focused on my academic studies, which I believed was the path I should follow.

Looking back now, I realize that the Holy Spirit gently reminded me to return to my ministry position to pursue music and continue to write songs. Simultaneously, I discovered immense joy in being involved in the youth choir, singing solos at church, and participating in school talent shows, allowing me to showcase my vocal abilities fully.

***

In the same year, 2015, I crossed paths with a remarkable young girl named Erica from Taiwan. She immediately caught my attention with a reserved personality and impeccable style. We were both enrolled in a unique program that allowed 10th and 11th-grade students to learn together, which was an excellent opportunity for both of us.

During that time, I found myself struggling with various subjects in class. Math, science, and even literature posed challenges I couldn't overcome alone. Fortunately, Erica came into my life like a guiding light. She was academically gifted and had an incredible ability to explain complex concepts in a way that made them easy to grasp.

When we started studying together, Erica became my mentor and friend. We spent countless hours in the class period reviewing textbooks, solving equations, and dissecting passages. She approached each topic with patience and an unwavering determination to help me understand. Her guidance improved my grades, boosted my confidence, and made me believe in my potential.

What struck me most about Erica was her genuine kindness and willingness to go the extra mile. She never hesitated to lend a hand, even when it meant sacrificing her study time. Whenever I stumbled upon an unfamiliar concept, she patiently broke it down into smaller, more manageable parts until I grasped the underlying principles.

Beyond academics, we shared many beautiful memories during our high school years. We formed a memorable bond from participating in extracurricular activities to attending school events. Erica's presence radiated warmth and positivity, making every experience all the more enjoyable.

Years have passed since our last encounter, but Erica remains a cherished friend in my heart. I often wonder how she's doing and hope life has been kind to her. Regardless of where she is now, I know her impact on my life will forever be imprinted in my memories.

Looking back, my high school years hold a significant place in my heart, mainly due to

Erica's presence. Her kindness, intelligence, and unwavering support transformed my academic journey and taught me invaluable life lessons. I will forever be grateful for our unique learning experience and her profound impact on my life.

What struck me most about Erica was her genuine kindness and willingness to go the extra mile. She never hesitated to lend a hand, even when it meant sacrificing her study time. Whenever I stumbled upon an unfamiliar concept, she patiently broke it down into smaller, more manageable parts until I grasped the underlying principles.

In the following year, 2016, In 11th grade, my life took a memorable turn when I found myself in the presence of Adja, a cheerful young lady with an unruly personality. Adja's unique blend of humor and tenderness drew me towards her. Our friendship was forged through our after-school routine of solving math problems and assisting each other with other subjects. One thing that stood out about Adja was her relentless commitment to her academics.

Together, Adja and I would head to the library across the street, armed with textbooks and determination to conquer the enigma that was math. Our shared classes ensured that studying together became effortless. This bond made learning enjoyable and encouraged us to push our limits.

Witnessing Adja's growth brought me immense joy. She strived diligently to excel in her studies, often going the extra mile to tackle complex problems. Her infectious enthusiasm spread to me, motivating me to put my best foot forward. I found solace and inspiration in her company, allowing me to explore my potential.

Adja's wild personality kept our study sessions vibrant. Amidst equations and formulas, laughter echoed through the library as we unraveled the intricacies of numbers. Her ability to infuse humor into our academic pursuits made learning math seem lighter and more manageable.

However, behind Adja's witty exterior, I discovered a softer side. At times, she would confide in me about her fears and doubts. I became her sounding board in those moments, offering a listening ear and reassurance. Our friendship went beyond mere academic collaboration; it became a constant support system for both of us.

As our time in 10th and 11th grade grew close, I reflected on our shared growth and experiences. Adja's determination and lightheartedness helped her excel academically and impacted my educational journey. Our time together has reminded us of the significance of hard work, camaraderie, and finding joy in pursuing knowledge.

Looking back now, I cherish the memories of our afternoons in the library, where we conquered math problems, shared laughter, and supported each other through thick and thin. Adja's influence on my life during our 10th and 11th-grade years remains imprinted in my mind, reminding me of the power of friendship, dedication, and the potential to achieve great things.

Indeed, I will forever be grateful for the privilege of knowing Adja and her impact on my life. Through our shared experiences, she reminded me that the path to success is not solitary but is built upon the foundation of collaboration, resilience, and genuine connection.

> Together, Adja and I would head to the library across the street, armed with textbooks and determination to conquer the enigma that was math. Our shared classes ensured that studying together became effortless. This bond made learning enjoyable and encouraged us to push our limits.

AMID MY QUESTIONABLE EXISTENCE

***

In the bustling city of New York, a prestigious institution, Manhattan International High School. It was within the hallowed halls of this school that my high school journey began, a journey fraught with many challenges and triumphs. Reflecting upon those formative years, I am reminded of the numerous ups and downs that tested my emotional, physical, and spiritual fortitude.

In the realm of emotions, I found myself grappling with a sea of inner turmoil, battling demons that no one else could see. The weight of these struggles threatened to engulf me in a relentlessly dark abyss. However, amidst the turbulent waves, I discovered an unexpected lifeline: support from friends, staff members, and fellow students. Their unwavering belief in me shone like a beacon, guiding me toward the shore of hope and resilience.

During the times when I descended into the depths of depression, I adeptly concealed my inner battles from prying eyes. My facade of strength painted a picture of normalcy, shielding those around me from the storm that raged within. In solitude, I sought solace in the ordinary, finding respite in minor activities, such as engaging in class projects or physical education classes.

Gym class became my sanctuary, a realm where I could momentarily cast aside my burdens and immerse myself in the world of movement. Though I could not fully participate due to the weight of my emotional episodes, I discovered immeasurable joy and inspiration by witnessing my peers engage in various games and sports. Their laughter echoed through the vast halls as they ran, jumped, and competed, reminding me of the vitality and resilience that lay dormant within me.

It is with deep gratitude that I recall the unwavering support I received from those who walked alongside me throughout my high school journey. Each interaction with friends, staff members, and fellow students provided a glimmer of hope, reaffirming my belief in the intrinsic goodness present in our society. We formed an unbreakable bond, united by our shared goal of crossing the finish line and embracing the culmination of our high school years.

Standing here, on the edge of a new chapter, I am filled with a profound sense of accomplishment. The highs and lows that marked my time at Manhattan International High School have sculpted me into a resilient individual capable of weathering the storms that life may bring. The memories of laughter, perseverance, and camaraderie will forever be etched into the tapestry of my heart.

Looking back, my high school years were a testament to the undeniable power of human connection and support. Through the turmoil and triumphs that defined this chapter of my life, I have emerged stronger, wiser, and ready to face whatever lies beyond. My heartfelt appreciation goes out to those who played a vital role in shaping me into the person I am today, proving that even amidst the darkest nights, there is always a glimmer of hope to guide us toward the light.

***

At Manhattan International High School, a young boy named Yumin hailed from Taiwan. Yumin was a quiet and introverted young guy, always lost in his thoughts. Despite this, he possessed a brilliant intellect, and his sharp mind often amazed those around him. He rarely spoke in our classroom's Bermuda Triangle of noise and chatter, but his silent presence was comforting and inspiring.

We were both in the same class in 11th grade at the prestigious Manhattan International High School. Yumin's reserved nature connected with my introverted personality, yet we found common ground in our love for learning. Yumin never hesitated to lend a helping hand whenever I struggled to understand our class materials' complexities. Patiently, he would unravel the mysteries, enlightening me with his profound insights. His assistance was a lifeline, and I always felt grateful for his presence.

However, fate had a different plan for Yumin. On a winter's morning, when the frigid breeze pierced through the bustling corridors, I felt an urgent need to answer nature's call and excused myself from the class under the watchful eye of our teacher, Ms. Darlene. As I approached the bathroom door, a peculiar sight caught my attention in the hallway.

There stood Yumin, his face adorned with determination and sadness. To my surprise, he was accompanied by our school's principal, Ms. Gladys. Intrigued and concerned, I approached the bathroom door. It was evident that something significant was transpiring—a turning point in Yumin's life.

Confusion clouded my thoughts as I tried to comprehend the scene unfolding before me. I didn't know then that Yumin was leaving Manhattan International High School due to unforeseen circumstances. The weight of thoughts keeps sinking deep into my mind and heart.

Without knowing or understanding what was happening, that encounter in the hallway would be my last glimpse of Yumin. I was still trying to understand why and what happened to him or the reasons behind his departure. I pondered his sudden disappearance for years, wondering where life had taken him. What had become of that brilliant mind and silent devotion to education? The unanswered questions haunted me relentlessly, weaving a tapestry of curiosity.

The years of wondering turned into an unbreakable thread of hope as time passed. I fervently hoped that Yumin was living a life filled with happiness and success, wherever he may be. Perhaps he had chosen a path that allowed his genius to flourish or embarked on a thrilling adventure that embraced his quiet nature. Whatever the case, I imagined him navigating through life's challenges with the same resilience and determination I witnessed that day in the hallway.

Now, as I sit here reminiscing, the

memories of Yumin continue to inspire me. His silent presence and unwavering support taught me the power of empathy and understanding. I have often questioned whether he ever knew the profound impact he had on my life, shaping me into a better version of myself.

> Confusion clouded my thoughts as I tried to comprehend the scene unfolding before me. I didn't know then that Yumin was leaving Manhattan International High School due to unforeseen circumstances. The weight of thoughts keeps sinking deep into my mind and heart.
>
> I was waiting in line to print my papers at the Fiterman Hall Library of Borough of Manhattan Community College when I saw a

familiar figure. To my surprise, it was Yumin! He looked like he was doing well. Sadly, that was the last time I saw him.

So, wherever you are, Yumin, know that your legacy lives on in the hearts of those whose lives you touched. Your intelligence and kindness continue to shine as a beacon of inspiration. As the seasons change and time carries us forward, I hope our paths will cross again one day, allowing me to express my gratitude and share stories of how your influence endured.

May you always find solace and success, dear Yumin.

***

While my days were primarily spent engrossed in various subjects at school, a part of me yearned to pursue this passion for music. It was a constant battle between the practicality of academic pursuits and the fulfillment found in following my singing aspirations. However, despite my uncertainty, I began acknowledging the significance of this unyielding pull towards music.

The more I immersed myself in choir rehearsals and performances, the more I realized my love for singing was not simply a passing fancy. Singing became an integral part of my identity, and I understood that it was meant to be nurtured and celebrated.

Every time I stepped onto the stage, my heart raced with a unique blend of nerves and excitement. The spotlight was mine, and I was ready to give my all. The audience's applause and encouragement fueled a fire, reaffirming my belief that music was my purpose.

Gradually, I started seeking opportunities beyond the confines of my school and church. I eagerly participated in local talent competitions and auditions, immersing myself in the competitive world of music. The journey was not without hurdles, but I grew more robust and determined to succeed with each challenge.

As the years unfolded, my conviction in pursuing my passion for singing intensified. I gained confidence in my abilities and began investing more time into honing my craft. I sought guidance from seasoned professionals and enrolled in vocal training programs, absorbing every piece of advice and technique.

With persistence and sheer dedication, I embarked on an incredible musical journey that took me beyond the confines of my high school and into the broader realm of the performing arts. The path could have been smoother, and there were moments of doubt and hesitation. However, I always found solace in the joy that singing brought to my life and the connection it allowed me to establish with my audience.

Looking back, I am deeply grateful for the Holy Spirit's silent nudges and the determination that led me back to my true calling. My studies were undeniably critical, but they always supported the fulfillment and purpose I found in pursuing my passion for singing.

Today, as I reflect upon my journey, I find myself in a position where I can inspire others with my music. Through my experiences, both triumphs and failures, I understand the transformative power of following one's heart and embracing the beauty of one's talents.

At last, my story is a testament to the profound impact that music has had on my life. It is a celebration of dreams pursued, obstacles overcome, and the joy of embracing one's true calling.

In the year 2016 transition and preparation, I found myself transitioning to 11th grade at Manhattan International High School. It was a pivotal moment as a student as I began to prepare for my college entrance and explore the possibilities for my future career.

As I started exploring college paths. I embarked on this journey; I felt excitement and uncertainty. The world of higher education seemed vast and overwhelming, with countless options and approaches. I knew that my decisions this year would significantly impact my future.

To seek guidance and clarity, I better understood the various career options and sought advice from my teachers, mentors, and counselors. They helped me explore different fields of study and encouraged me to reflect on my passions, strengths, and goals.

On my journey to embrace self-discovery, during this time, I actively engaged in self-reflection and self-discovery. I delved into my interests, hobbies, and subjects that sparked my curiosity. Through this process, I began uncovering my true passions and strengths, which helped me narrow my potential career choices.

While my time as a high school student was almost ending, I had to do the following. In addition to exploring my career options, I also dedicated myself to preparing for college entrance exams. I attended study groups, sought additional resources, and worked diligently to improve my academic skills. The long hours of studying and preparation were challenging, but I knew they were essential for my future success.

As the year ended, I felt a sense of accomplishment and clarity. While I may not have had all the answers, I have taken significant steps toward understanding myself and my future aspirations. The journey of self-discovery and college preparation had only begun, but I was determined to continue exploring and working toward my dreams.

And so, armed with newfound knowledge and a sense of purpose, I eagerly stepped into the next chapter of my educational journey, ready to embrace the challenges and opportunities ahead.

***

In the year 2016, I found myself sinking into the depths of depression and being haunted by constant thoughts of suicide. With each passing moment during the day, I seemed to amplify these dark emotions that relentlessly consumed my mind. These unwelcome visitors invaded my mind relentlessly, invading every moment of my day. During this darkness, my family and I resided in a humble yet towering 20-

floor apartment nestled within the colossal structure of the 30 River Road building.

It was during the afternoons and nights when these suicidal thoughts would overpower me as if urging me to leap into the abyss below. My emotions were in disarray, leaving me unable to untangle the knots of anger within me. I would scream and rage, unable to find solace or peace amidst the turmoil that consumed me. Desperate for a change, my mother would continuously pray for my heart to soften and for my anger to dissipate.

After every attempt I've made in my mind, I realized that committing suicide was an unforgivable sin after constant prayers to seek peace and help from above. Just as I emerged from the depths of despair, remember that within you lies an indomitable spirit ready to overcome any obstacle that stands in your way.

But as fate would have it, a remarkable transformation began to unfold within me two years later. It was as if a celestial force touched my weary soul, leading me to embark on a spiritual journey. I started to pray, not just for inner peace but also for the presence of Jesus to enter and heal my wounded heart. This newfound faith became a guiding light amidst my struggles, including the battle to stay focused in school.

Though the weight of depression made it difficult to concentrate, I persevered and managed to complete my academic semester at High School. It was a testament to the strength I discovered within myself and the unwavering support of my loved ones. Through sheer determination, I continued to fight against the tides of darkness threatening to drown me.

As I immersed myself in prayer and sought divine intervention, I witnessed a remarkable change within me. The burdens weighing me down gradually lifted, unveiling glimpses of hope and purpose. As I embraced my renewed faith, the once-dreary world seemed vibrant and full of possibilities.

Through these trials, I learned that even the darkest moments have the potential for a glimmer of light. I discovered the power of prayer, not only in the intercession of a devoted mother but within myself as well. The journey towards self-discovery and healing may be fraught with challenges, but it is through these very struggles that our true strength is revealed.

AMID MY QUESTIONABLE EXISTENCE

***

At Manhattan International High School, I used to immerse myself in various extracurricular activities after school. Among the options, one action filled me with the utmost joy: singing. Every year, our school hosted a highly anticipated talent show, and it was during these cherished moments I got to share my gift with the world.

As the curtains would rise, my heart would flutter in anticipation of the warm reception that awaited me. The stage lights would illuminate the room, casting a magical glow that enveloped the crowd. The air would be thick with anticipation and excitement, setting the stage for an unforgettable evening.

With my vocal cords tuned and my emotions soaring, I would take center stage. The microphone, an extension of my being, would rest against my lips, ready to release a harmonious and melodic symphony. As the first note left my mouth, a hush would fall over the room, a testament to the power of music to captivate hearts.

Through my performance, I could touch my classmates' souls. The sheer joy and appreciation that radiated from their faces was enough to fuel my passion even further. Each verse and each chorus became more than just a series of musical notes strung together; they became a message, a connection forged between souls in that fleeting moment.

Yet, sometimes, I chose not to participate in the talent show, to sit back and let others take the spotlight. In those instances, Rachel, a dear friend of mine, would inevitably approach me with a sparkle in her eyes. "Aren't you going to sing this time?" she would ask earnestly. "Please sing for us. We love seeing you perform!" Caught off guard by her sincere request, I could only muster a shy smile and reply, "Oh, maybe next year. I promise I'll enchant your ears and hearts once more."

True to my word, as each year passed, I diligently prepared myself for the next round of the talent show. I honed my skills, explored new genres, and poured my heart into refining my craft. Every practice session brought me closer to delivering a performance that would leave an indelible mark on the hearts of those who listened.

And when the time finally arrived, with anticipation coursing through my veins, I took to the stage again. The familiar faces of my peers watched with bated breath as my first notes cascaded through the air. This time, I sang with newfound confidence, allowing my voice to soar beyond the confines of the auditorium.

The applause from the crowd was music to my ears, a resounding affirmation of their unwavering support. At that moment, I knew I had fulfilled my promise to both them and me. Their smiles and cheers inspired me to continue pursuing my passion for singing, sharing my voice, and touching lives through melodies.

As I walked off the stage, my heart brimming with joy, A young girl approached me with a happy smile. "You have no idea how beautiful your voice is," she whispered. "Thank you for keeping your promise and gracing us with your talent. Your voice brings light to our souls." I couldn't help but return her happiness with the happiness of my own, for it was in that fleeting exchange that I realized the true power of music: its ability to transcend boundaries and forge connections.

From that day forward, I knew that no matter where life took me, I would never abandon my love for singing. The memories created on that Manhattan International High School stage would forever hold a special place in my heart, a reminder of the incredible journey I had embarked upon.

And so, armed with renewed determination and an unwavering spirit, I ventured into a future brimming with endless opportunities. I carried the echoes of that talent show within me, forever grateful for its impact on my life. Each day, I continued to embrace my love for singing, sharing my soul through every note and inspiring others to follow their dreams.

For in that small corner of the world, at Manhattan International High School, where dreams harmonized, and talents flourished, a mere promise turned into a symphony that resonated far beyond the confines of those hallowed halls.

While continuing my studies at Manhattan International High School, I couldn't help but sense a persistent, nagging feeling deep in my heart. It whispered to me, urging me to pursue my passion for singing. Yet, despite this inner longing, I was unsure how and where to start. Determined to prioritize my academic studies, I pushed aside these thoughts and focused solely on my textbooks and assignments. Looking back now, I am convinced it was the gentle prodding of the Holy Spirit nudging me back toward my ministry position.

However, a newfound joy emerged in my life as time went on. I discovered immense satisfaction and fulfillment in being involved in the youth choir at my church. The energy and enthusiasm of the other choir members fueled my excitement and renewed my love for singing. Within the safe embrace of this spirited community, I was encouraged to explore my vocal range, experiment with harmonies, and grow as a performer.

Emboldened by these experiences, I took a leap of faith and decided to showcase my gifted voice by singing solo at church services. The support and encouragement from my fellow churchgoers fortified my confidence and spurred me to improve. Their unwavering belief in my talent ignited a flickering flame of hope, reassuring me that perhaps my dream of pursuing a singing career wasn't as far-fetched as I had once believed......

The next opportunity to prove myself came when my high school announced its annual talent show. With trembling hands, I signed up to participate, determined to demonstrate my abilities to friends and teachers. As I stood on the stage, facing a sea of expectant faces, I felt apprehension and excitement surging through my veins. With each note that escaped my lips, I poured my soul into the performance, allowing music to become the conduit through which my emotions flowed.

***

On a warm afternoon in 2017, an unusual sensation seized my body, leaving me paralyzed and helpless. I found myself lying down in the living room, unable to move, yet still fully conscious. Panic surged through my veins as I desperately tried to understand what had befallen me. My mind raced, searching for answers amidst the darkness that consumed me.

As fate would have it, my mother emerged from her bedroom, her eyes widening in shock as they landed upon my motionless figure. She rushed to my side, concern etched across her face, her heart filled with worry and determination. With trembling hands, she gently caressed my cheek, trying to understand the depth of my predicament.

But my mother, a woman of unwavering faith and infinite strength, refused to let despair find a home within her heart. She knelt beside me, and at that moment, her prayers resonated with an enthusiasm that surpassed any prior plea. She prayed with words and all the emotions she carried within her: frustration, anger, and above all, an overwhelming sense of determination that cried out, "Enough is enough!"

Her prayers rose like a symphony of hope, echoing throughout the room. Each word carried the weight of her love and longing as if she was willing the universe itself to hear her plea. In a profound moment of connection between mother and child, her prayer became an anthem of resilience in the face of adversity.

And then, like a divine whisper from above, strength coursed through my body. Inch by inch, I regained control over my limbs until I finally stood upright. As I could see the sadness on my mother's face, my mother's eyes almost welled up with tears of profound gratitude, realizing our unyielding devotion had brought this miraculous transformation.

Overwhelmed with a deep sense of gratitude and blessed relief, we locked eyes as a unified force. In that profound connection, we knew our journey together had reached a pivotal moment. We both understood the power of faith, the significance of unwavering love, and the unfathomable support that prayers can bring.

Together, we clasped hands and knelt again, this time not in desperation but in solidarity. With voices filled with reverence, we thanked God for granting us this immense blessing. Our prayer became a symphony of gratitude, a melody of appreciation, and an elegy for our previous struggles.

From that moment onward, life took on a different hue. Every step I took, every breath I drew, became a testament to the power of love and prayer. The memory of that fateful afternoon is forever etched within our hearts, reminding us that faith and determination can pave the way for transformation even in the face of seemingly insurmountable obstacles.

As years passed and the memory of that day slowly melded into the tapestry of our lives, such an event never occurred again. Yet, the lessons learned remained steadfast, guiding us through life's labyrinthine pathways. The bond between a mother and child grew stronger, forever fortified by the shared experience of conquering adversity hand in hand.

And so, as I recount this story today, I am reminded of the incredible power that lies within us all. In the face of darkness, when we feel lost or powerless, our unwavering conviction and steadfast belief in a greater force can ignite the flame of resilience. May this tale serve as a beacon of hope and a testament to the extraordinary strength within the human spirit.

***

One of the most anticipated events in this esteemed institution was the annual celebration known as Culture Day, or International Day, as we affectionately referred to it. It was a day when each student brought forth a piece of their heritage, proudly showcasing their country's flavors through delectable dishes prepared with love and tradition.

From the moment I stepped into the hallowed halls of Manhattan International High School as a bright-eyed freshman, I yearned to participate in this vibrant celebration. Each passing year brought me closer to my goal, and anticipation swelled as I eagerly awaited my chance to be part of this grand culinary extravaganza.

Finally, that day arrived when I entered my sophomore year, and the atmosphere pulsated with boundless excitement. Preparations for International Day began months in advance, with students diligently researching their ancestral recipes and perfecting their culinary skills under their family's watchful gaze.

As 9th graders, we watched in awe as our seniors mesmerized us with their diverse dishes. The auditorium transformed into a global banquet hall, where tantalizing aromas wafted. We feasted fragrant curries from India, savory empanadas from Argentina, aromatic tagines from Morocco, and sumptuous sushi rolls from Japan. The melting pot of flavors unraveled the rich tapestry of our collective heritage.

The following year, armed with newfound knowledge and a burning passion to share my cultural delights, I embarked on this enchanting culinary journey. Days turned into nights as I pored over ancient recipes passed down through generations. Guided by the wisdom of my ancestors, I delicately crafted a masterpiece that would carry the spirit of my homeland.

When International Day finally arrived, the school became a bustling bazaar. Each hallway was adorned with colorful flags, representing the diverse nations flourishing within the school's embrace. Excitement reverberated through the crowd as students bustled about, their dishes adorned with pride and tradition.

I laid my contribution on a splendid table, meticulously garnished and infused with various spices that spoke of my cultural heritage. Beside me stood countless others, their faces radiant with joy and anticipation. Our dishes whispered tales of distant lands, bridging the gap between nations and fostering a deeper understanding and appreciation for one another.

As visitors roamed from country to country, their senses were immersed in a kaleidoscope of flavors and aromas. Conversations danced between the mingling cultures, learning about customs and traditions that expanded our horizons. It was a celebration that transcended boundaries and showcased the immense power of unity amidst diversity.

I continued this remarkable journey year after year, eagerly embracing each Culture Day with renewed vigor and exhilaration. The memories created during those enchanting days became indelible imprints on my heart, forging bonds transcending borders and time.

At Manhattan International High School, Culture Day was the epitome of what education should be – a melting pot of ideas, experiences, and cuisines that enriched our minds and taste buds. It taught us that diversity was not a mere concept but a vibrant reality to be celebrated and cherished.

As I approached my final year at Manhattan International High School, I felt bittersweet nostalgia. The culmination of this extraordinary culinary adventure would be bitter as we bid farewell to our beloved school. However, the memories of these Culture Days will forever remain etched in our souls, reminding us of the power of unity and the beauty of celebrating our differences.

***

As the year of High School almost ends, I am from a remarkable institution, Manhattan International High School. I remember it being a place where dreams were forged, friendships blossomed, and diversity thrived. As I embarked on my journey through those hallowed halls, little did I know that this extraordinary school would leave an indelible mark on my life.

The school campus, full of vibrant cultures, greeted me from the moment I entered. Students from every corner of the globe converged in a melting pot of ideas and experiences. It was a symphony of languages, a tapestry of traditions, and a celebration of diversity. In the classrooms, discussions resonated with multiple perspectives as we learned from textbooks and each other. These encounters with students from all backgrounds broadened my horizons, fostering empathy and understanding that would serve me well beyond the confines of these walls.

While my academic performance at Manhattan International High School may not have been extraordinary, I was driven by an unwavering determination to pursue my educational goals. I discovered my true potential within those hallways and learned the value of hard work. Countless hours were spent pouring over textbooks, engaging in rigorous discussions, and wrestling with complex equations. Every challenge was seen as an opportunity for growth, a stepping stone towards academic excellence.

Amidst this pursuit of knowledge, there came a pivotal moment when I was introduced to one of the most remarkable teachers I have ever encountered – Ms. Lindsay. Her effervescent aura enveloped the classroom from the first day I met her. With her infectious enthusiasm and zest for teaching, she breathed life into even the dreariest subjects. In her presence, learning became an adventure, a captivating journey of exploration. Ms. Lindsay turned abstract theories into tangible realities, igniting a fire within me that continues to burn brightly.

Not only did Ms. Lindsay inspire me, but the bond we forged became an unwavering pillar of support throughout my high school years. As my assistant teacher, she imbued me with the confidence to overcome academic obstacles and pushed me beyond my perceived limitations. Through her guidance, I discovered hidden talents and developed skills I never thought possible. Ms. Lindsay's genuine care and unwavering belief in my abilities propelled me toward success.

Yet it wasn't just the teachers who profoundly shaped my experience at Manhattan

International High School. Gratitude emanates from my heart for the fellow students who joined me on this arduous yet rewarding journey. We supported each other through late-night study sessions, collaborative projects, and heartfelt conversations, inspiring growth and personal development. These friendships forged amidst the shared joys and challenges will forever hold a special place within me.

As I stand at the precipice of a new chapter in my life, fond memories of Manhattan International High School flicker across the canvas of my mind. It was a place where diversity was embraced, hard work was valued, and excellence was pursued. It was a haven of support, nurturing dreams, and fostering character. From the vibrant hallways to the buzzing classrooms, every corner held a story etched deep within my soul.

Thank you, Manhattan International High School, for the years we shared. The memories we created will always be cherished, and the lessons learned will forever treasured. As I venture into the world with knowledge, resilience, and a global outlook, I know your spirit will forever guide my steps. I am forever grateful for your impact on me and the indomitable place you hold within my heart.

There were so many memories of Manhattan International High School that had a lot of impact on me. I first got to meet students from all backgrounds. We shared so many great memories. Aside from that, my academic performance was okay. I worked hard to achieve my educational goals. I remember being introduced to one of the most outstanding teachers for the first time the year I entered. Her name was Lindsay; I called her Ms. Lindsay, a young woman with a fun and energetic aura, I believe it was either 10th or 11th grade, who would be my assistant teacher for the rest of my High school years. I am grateful to have the extra support of a few students I worked with. Thank you, Manhattan International High School, for the wonderful years we've shared. You'll forever be in my heart.

AMID MY QUESTIONABLE EXISTENCE

The year 2017 was the saddest year of my life, one that I never thought would bring so much pain and turmoil to my family. It all began with the shocking revelation that my father had been having an affair with his mistress. This heart-wrenching betrayal tore our family apart, leaving us abandoned and broken.

The news of my father's infidelity spread like wildfire, reaching every corner of our lives. It appears the whole world knew what had happened, from the government officials to the people on social media. Even those remotely connected to our family were aware of the scandal.

The weight of this knowledge was unbearable. Our once tight-knit family was now shattered, left to pick up the pieces of our broken hearts. The pain we felt was immeasurable, and the shame we carried was immense.

Amid this chaos, we found solace in each other. We leaned on one another for support, finding strength in the bonds of love that held us together. Despite the darkness, we vowed to rise above it and rebuild our lives.

As time passed, wounds slowly began to heal. We learned to forgive, not for our father's sake, but for our peace of mind. We realized that holding onto anger and resentment would only prolong our suffering.

Though the scars of that fateful year will always remain, we emerged from the darkness more robust and resilient. We learned the value of family and the importance of cherishing those we hold dear.

2017 may have been the saddest year of my life, but it became a turning point. It taught me the power of forgiveness, the strength of love, and the resilience of the human spirit. And as we move forward, we carry these lessons with us, knowing that we can overcome any adversity that comes our way.

My final senior year of 2017 at Manhattan International High School was the year in my life as a student when I started to prepare for my official college entrance. It was a time to act and work on finalizing all the steps I had taken throughout my academic journey.

As the end of the school year approached, I dedicated myself to working on my final academic project. It culminated all the knowledge and skills I had acquired over the years. The project was a test of my intellectual abilities and a reflection of my growth as a student.

I spent countless hours researching, writing, and revising. The project became my obsession, consuming my thoughts and energy. There were moments of frustration and self-doubt, but I pushed through, determined to make it the best possible.

The support of my teachers and classmates was invaluable during this time. They provided guidance, feedback, and encouragement, reminding me I was not alone in this journey. Together, we navigated the challenges and celebrated the victories.

As the school year ended, I felt a sense of accomplishment and relief. I had completed my final academic project and was ready to embark on the next chapter of my life. The hard work and dedication had paid off, and I was excited about the future.

Looking back, the final year of high school was a transformative period. It was a time of growth, both academically and personally. I learned the importance of perseverance and the value of collaboration. Most importantly, I discovered I could overcome challenges with determination and a robust support system.

As I prepare to enter college, I carry the lessons I learned during that final year with me. I am confident in my abilities and excited for the opportunities. The last year may have been filled with hard work and uncertainty, but it also shaped me into who I am today.

I want to thank all the staff and teachers who were there with me from 9th to 12th grade. Principal Gladys Dorilda Rodrigues, former principal Mr. Alan Krull. Faculty and Staff: Ms. Daria Olivero, Ms. Allison Finiasz, Ms. Madeline Gonzales, Ms. Willie Rabalais, Ms. Bogumila Snihur, Ms. Wioleta Metel, Mr. James Barkley, and Ms. Rui Qiu Ye Liu. Foundations (9th): Mr. Moses Ahn, Ms. Gallia Kassiano, and Ms. Marie McAnuff. Choice, Actions, Reflection (CAR), and Innovation Transformation (10th & 11th): Ms. Darlene Murphy, Ms. Lindsay Lyons, Mr. Brian Wasserman, and Ms. Athena Theodoris. Achievers (12th): Ms. Luz

Dará Valconcha, Ms. Yanira Roman, Mr. Richard Perrone, Ms. Cinzia Bontempo, Ms. Bonnie MacSavenly, and Mr. Martin Pascual. To the other teachers who were not part of my journey as one of their students, I would also love to extend my gratitude for their excellent teaching. Mr. Felix Colon, Ms. Jane Lawrence, Mr. Mathew Kennedy, Mr. Zachary Klurfeld, Mr. Lenny Melzer, Ms. Andrea Kassiano, Ms. Nina Kogut-Akkum, and Ms. Kholood Qumei. Thank you all for your magnificent teaching.

Reflecting upon the years I spent studying at Manhattan International High School, I realize it was one of my life's most tremendously transformative moments.

AMID MY QUESTIONABLE EXISTENCE

I am grateful for all the people that I've met during my time there. The friendships I made, the teachers who guided me, and my experiences all contributed to shaping the person I am today.

Manhattan International High School provided a multicultural environment that enriched my world understanding. Interacting with students from diverse backgrounds broadened my perspective and taught me to appreciate different cultures and traditions.

The school's commitment to academic excellence pushed me to strive for greatness. The dedicated teachers encouraged me to explore my passions and think critically. They instilled in me a love for learning that inspires me today.

AMID MY QUESTIONABLE EXISTENCE

As I bid farewell to Manhattan International High School, I carry the memories of laughter, growth, and personal development. I am confident that the friends I made and the lessons I learned will continue to impact my life wherever I go.

So, here's to the incredible journey at Manhattan International High School and all the fantastic people who have crossed my path. May we all continue to thrive and make a positive difference in the world, no matter where our paths may lead us.

> I also want to extend my sincere gratitude to my fellow class of 2017 for your conditional supports; Ahmed A, Hassan A, Hesham A, Haggur A, Mamadou B, Karina B, Johanna B, Maria B, Joshua B,

Leslie C, Nikerson C, Franny L.D, Enyi R.D, Amatoulaye D, Mamadou D, Sange D, David E, Domenica E, Fares E, Yara E, Mohammed E, Moises E, Ivan E, Syed F, Nicole F, Nayelis G, Jeisy B.G, Mouhamaddo G, Jerry G, Ishan G, Wiliana G, Patrycja H, Bibi J, Esmeralda P.J, Patience K, Rinchen L, Saleha L, Hamderfford P.L, Yarelis M, Franci D.M, Martinez M, Rene M, Hezam M, Wandy R.M, Adja N, Maimouna N, Nathalia N, Bartlomiej O, Bayron P, Genesis P, Kristian P, Atiqur R, Kevin R, Orline S, Seydina S, Sadaf S, Melvin S, Arisara S, Alaa T, Hawa T, Daba T, Pathe P.T, Paulina T, Nimsy V, Aye H.W, Abu W, and Gebrela Z.

AMID MY QUESTIONABLE EXISTENCE

It was 2017, and I had just graduated high school with excitement and anticipation for the next chapter of my life. Eager to get a head start on my college journey, I enrolled in a College Now - Math class before officially starting my academic year in the spring semester of 2018.

As the gentle breeze carried the scent of blooming flowers, I stepped into my new classroom with nerves and determination. Little did I know that this class would shape my mathematical understanding and bring unexpected turns to my personal life.

During that spring semester, an unforeseen twist of fate struck my family and me. Due to unforeseen circumstances, we were notified that we had to move from our cozy apartment in Roosevelt Island to a new place at

33rd Street and Second Avenue in the bustling Midtown East of Manhattan. This sudden upheaval turned our lives upside down as we grappled with relocation challenges amidst our academic endeavors.

Leaving behind the familiarity of Roosevelt Island, where we had grown accustomed to its tight-knit community and serene atmosphere, took time. However, we embraced the opportunity for change with resilient hearts, ready to forge new memories in the heart of Manhattan.

Our new abode awaited us at one towering building, Kips Bay Towers. We felt awe as we entered the grand lobby adorned with plush furnishings and gleaming marble floors. We were now part of a vibrant community that would shape our experiences in this remarkable city.

Embracing the rhythm of bustling streets and towering skyscrapers, I felt invigorated by the energy that surged through Midtown East. The once-familiar sights of Roosevelt Island were replaced by the vivacity of Times Square, Central Park's green expanse, and the iconic Empire State Building, standing tall like a guardian of my newfound dreams.

Yet, amidst the excitement of the city's pulse, I longed for the simplicity and tranquility of Roosevelt Island. As days turned into weeks, I found solace in exploring new spaces with my little sibling, who shared my worries and adventures. Together, we walked through Central Park's winding trails, discovering hidden corners that offered respite from the urban clamor. Our laughter echoed through these lush landscapes as we reminisced about our times on Roosevelt Island.

The Math class that initially seemed like a mere stepping stone toward college opened doors I never expected. Within those walls, friendships blossomed as we navigated the intricacies of equations and formulas. My classmates became my allies in both mathematical triumphs and moments of bewilderment. Their support and camaraderie formed an unbreakable bond that transcended numerical calculations.

Through this immersive experience, I realized that life's unexpected directions often lead to remarkable moments of growth and discovery. My journey from Roosevelt Island to Midtown East taught me to adapt, to find beauty in change, and to treasure the connections forged along the way. It reminded me that while the destination may change, the spirit within us remains resilient and ready to seize new opportunities.

As the spring semester ended, I looked back at my time in the Math class with gratitude. It prepared me for the academic challenges that awaited and fostered personal growth that would shape my future endeavors. With newfound resilience and an indomitable spirit, I eagerly awaited the official start of my college journey, knowing that the unpredictable twists of life would only bring greater depth and richness to my story.

AMID MY QUESTIONABLE EXISTENCE

***

2018, I officially started as a college student at Borough of Manhattan Community College - The City University of New. As a determined young lady, I embarked on a journey filled with colossal challenges and overwhelming obstacles in the bustling streets of New York City at the renowned Borough of Manhattan Community College. Little did I know that it was through the boundless grace of God that I would overcome these trials and ultimately achieve her hard-earned academic success.

As a bright and ambitious student, I arrived at Borough of Manhattan Community College with dreams as vast as the city's skyline. I had set my sights on obtaining my associate degree, a path I believed would pave the way for a promising future. However, unbeknownst to me, this undertaking would prove to be nothing short of an arduous adventure.

From the first day, I was immersed in an academic whirlwind, faced with demanding coursework, rigorous schedules, and relentless deadlines. The weight of this newfound responsibility threatened to crush my spirit, leaving me feeling disheartened and overwhelmed. Nevertheless, I refused to succumb to defeat.

Days turned into weeks, weeks into months, and months into years as I bravely fought against the countless impediments that lay ahead. In these moments of despair, I found solace in her unwavering faith, clinging to the belief that I was not alone in this battle. Each day, my devotion grew stronger, igniting a flame of perseverance within my heart.

Even when financial burdens struck like a storm, threatening to sweep away my dreams, I found comfort in trusting my heavenly Father. I believed God would provide for my needs through unwavering faith and determination. With steadfast resolve, I sought assistance from scholarships, part-time jobs, and the helping hands of kind strangers who believed in my remarkable potential.

As I ventured into the intricate realm of academia, I encountered captivating lectures that sparked her intellectual curiosity. Professors became my guides, illuminating the path towards knowledge and enlightenment. However, there were times when seemingly insurmountable obstacles appeared, presenting themselves as difficult exams and intricate projects. These tests of will and intellect became battles to conquer, challenges that only the diligent and tenacious could withstand.

Yet I, firmly anchored by my unwavering belief in divine power, refused to let these trials diminish her spirit. I sought wisdom from my mentors and dedicated hours to endless studying, pushing beyond my limits to tap into the reservoirs of my potential. With each hurdle cleared, a newfound strength welled within me, as if God Himself had given me the wings I needed to soar.

Through four long years and one arduous month, I navigated the labyrinthine corridors of higher education, where every step forward seemed to be accompanied by two steps backward. Yet, neither exhaustion nor doubt deterred me from reaching my goal. Despite setbacks and sleepless nights, I embraced these hardships as stepping stones to the person I aspired to become.

***

Even through the most challenging time at Borough of Manhattan Community College, I always found the courage to be positive during my academic challenges. Pursuing higher education was never an easy journey for me, but it was a journey I was determined to embark upon.

As I mature, I face numerous obstacles on my path to success. The education system in my community was well-resourced; I was also one of the students who received the support they needed. Despite these challenges, I knew that education was my ticket to a better life, and I was determined to make the most of the opportunities that came my way.

When I entered the Borough of Manhattan Community College, I met a diverse and vibrant community of learners. The academic rigor demanded my utmost dedication and perseverance. The workload was overwhelming, and I often juggled multiple responsibilities to keep up with my coursework. Balancing my studies, a part-time job and family obligations was no easy feat, but I refused to let adversity define me.

Throughout my time at college, I encountered various setbacks. There were moments when self-doubt crept in, and I questioned whether I had what it took to succeed. However, I reminded myself of why I had embarked on this journey in the first place. I had a burning desire to break free from the poverty cycle and prove to myself and others that I could achieve my dreams.

In the face of adversity, I sought solace in a supportive network of friends, professors, and mentors. They provided me with guidance, cheered me on during moments of doubt, and reminded me of my potential. Their encouragement fueled my determination to persevere, even when the road ahead seemed impossible.

Every setback I encountered became an opportunity for growth. I learned to embrace my failures, viewing them as stepping stones towards success. I sought feedback from professors, constantly refining my approach to studying and learning. I discovered the power of time management and developed strategies to maximize my productivity.

Though the road was arduous, the countless hours spent studying and sacrificing paid off. I gradually began to excel academically, earning recognition for my achievements. But more importantly, I discovered a resilience within myself that I had never known before. I learned to stay positive, embrace challenges as opportunities for growth, and approach each hurdle with unwavering determination.

My experience at Borough of Manhattan Community College shaped me in profound ways. It taught me that success is not just measured by grades or accolades but by the strength of character developed in the face of adversity. It instilled in me a lifelong passion for learning and a hunger for knowledge that fuels my desire to make a difference in the world.

Today, as I reflect on my journey, I am proud of the person I have become. The obstacles I overcame during my time at Borough of Manhattan Community College have prepared me for the challenges that lie ahead. Armed with a positive mindset and an unwavering dedication to personal growth, I am confident that I can overcome any hurdle that comes my way.

My time at Borough of Manhattan Community College may have been fraught with challenges, but it was also a period of immense personal and academic growth. My story serves as a testament to the power of perseverance, resilience, and positivity in the face of adversity. I am grateful for the lessons learned and the person I have become.

In the same year of 2018, during the summer season 2018, my family and I embarked on a new chapter of our spiritual journey as we officially transferred to our new church location, the Manhattan Seventh Day Adventist Church. Situated in the vibrant borough of Manhattan, the church warmly welcomed us with open arms.

As we stepped into the church for the first time, I couldn't help but feel a sense of anticipation. The grandeur of the building and the peaceful atmosphere instilled a sense of reverence within me. It was here that we hoped to find not only a place of worship but also a community of like-minded individuals.

One person who had left an indelible mark on the congregation was our former pastor, Romeo. Sadly, he had passed away in the same year due to health issues. Despite the sadness that shrouded his departure, his memory continued in our hearts.

His unwavering belief in the power of love and unity made Pastor Romeo truly special. Every sermon he delivered was infused with these timeless values. Before delving into the depths of his message, he would warmly welcome all the visitors in attendance.

It was during these introductions that the spirit of unity indeed came alive. People from different walks of life, with varied backgrounds and beliefs, would stand up and share a part of themselves with the congregation. In those moments, the barriers that often divide us dissolved, and we were reminded that we were all on this spiritual journey together.

Pastor Romeo's words echoed in my mind as I reflected on that time. He believed proper spiritual growth could only be achieved through understanding and acceptance. And it was through these simple acts of welcoming and introducing ourselves we started to form genuine connections and build bridges within our church family.

Looking back, those introductions became more than just a formality. It was a way to break the ice, reach out to strangers, and make them feel valued. Every new face and story shared forged a more profound bond among the congregation.

As the years passed, our church in Manhattan continued to flourish. The seeds of love and unity planted by Pastor Romeo blossomed into a vibrant community where every member felt loved, appreciated, and included.

To this day, I carry with me the lessons taught by Pastor Romeo. His preaching of love and union remains integral to my spiritual journey. Whenever I step foot into our church, I am reminded of the power of introductions, the strength of unity, and the profound impact one person can have on a community.

As I recount my experience at the Manhattan Seventh Day Adventist Church, I am filled with gratitude for the warm welcome, the love, and the unity that has become the foundation of our faith. And I am reminded that the journey of faith isn't meant to be solitary but rather a shared experience of growth and togetherness.

At Manhattan Seventh Day Adventist Church, I was surrounded by a diverse group of young people above my age. It was an unexpected encounter that left a lasting impression on me. I first saw Mr. Kyron, the Young Adult (YA) program director. He passionately led our group, ensuring we would come together every afternoon for an enlightening Bible lesson.

Reflecting on those initial moments, I am filled with gratitude and pleasure. Witnessing young individuals gathering to worship our creator, God, was inspiring and humbling. The vibrant energy radiating from every member of the YA community fostered an atmosphere of profound spirituality and growth.

Mr. Kyron, with his unwavering dedication and wisdom, deftly steered the direction of our gatherings. He possessed an innate ability to engage each participant, igniting their enthusiasm for learning and spiritual development. His words held immense weight, resonating deep within our hearts and minds.

Under Mr. Kyron's guidance, the YA program transformed into a nurturing haven for everyone seeking spiritual nourishment. We embarked on a self-reflection journey, delving into our faith's teachings and discovering profound insights. Through lively discussions, thought-provoking lessons, and shared experiences, we grew as individuals and as a tightly-knit community.

The fellowship we shared extended beyond the walls of the church. We organized various outreach initiatives, engaging with the larger community and spreading the message of love and compassion. Together, we volunteered at homeless shelters, organized fundraising events for charitable causes, and participated in youth-led initiatives for positive change.

Our bond grew more robust as time passed, transcending our age differences. We celebrated each other's victories and lent a helping hand during difficult times. The Young Adult Program (YA) became an anchor in our lives, providing us with purpose, guidance, and cherished friendships.

Looking back, I realize the profound impact of being a part of this community on my life. It shaped my values, honed my character, and instilled a deep and lasting faith that continues to guide me today. I am forever grateful for the opportunity to have crossed paths with Mr. Kyron and the incredible young people I met at the Manhattan Seventh Day Adventist Church. They have forever left an indelible mark on my heart.

The Manhattan Seventh Day Adventist Church's YA program was transformative. I witnessed the power of faith, fellowship, and service through Mr. Kyron's leadership and the young participants' unwavering dedication. This autobiography is a testament to this community's profound influence on my life and the spiritual growth it instilled within me.

As a new Manhattan Seventh Day Adventist Church member, I honestly had the privilege of immersing myself in a diverse community of individuals from various cultures and backgrounds. While there, I became acquainted with the Manongi family, who hailed from Tanzania, my home country, and shared a similar purpose for being in the United States.

Attending the services at the church was always a delightful experience. The grandeur and beauty of the church building itself captivated my senses. It stood tall, an architectural masterpiece depicting the devotion and reverence of its congregants. The atmosphere inside was tranquil, inviting a sense of peace and spiritual serenity.

Within this spiritual sanctuary, I encountered people from all walks of life. Each person had a unique story to tell, and interacting with them enriched my understanding of the global tapestry of humanity. I had the opportunity to engage in meaningful conversations, expanding my knowledge about various cultures and traditions.

The Manongi family left an indelible mark on me. Their warmth, kindness, and familiarity made me feel right at home despite being thousands of miles away from Tanzania. They shared the same aspirations and challenges as I did, which created an instant connection. It was indeed comforting to find companionship in a foreign land.

The church community showcased their talents and displayed their cultural heritage during gatherings and events. We marveled at the vibrant dances, melodic music, and colorful attire representing the diverse backgrounds of the congregants. It was a visual feast celebrating the unity that transcended our differences.

Beyond the religious services, the church also offered opportunities to engage in community service. Together, we reached out to the less fortunate, providing food, shelter, and support to those in need. Witnessing the selflessness and generosity of my fellow church members was awe-inspiring. These acts of kindness further strengthened the bond we shared as a community.

Joining the Manhattan Seventh Day Adventist Church was a significant turning point. It allowed me to explore my faith, connect with individuals from diverse backgrounds, and find solace in a foreign land. The experiences I gained and my forged friendships will forever hold a cherished place in my heart.

Reflecting upon my time at the church, I am reminded of the power of unity and the beauty of embracing diversity. The Manhattan Seventh Day Adventist Church truly exemplified these values, fostering an environment of acceptance, love, and support. It is an experience that has shaped my worldview and will continue to guide me on my life's journey.

At the renowned Borough of Manhattan Community College, nestled amidst towering buildings and filled with ambitious students, I grappled with numerous academic challenges that seemed to collide with my personal life.

AMID MY QUESTIONABLE EXISTENCE

As a bright and vibrant soul, I had always dreamt of higher education and the opportunities it could bring me. However, life dealt me an unexpected hand as personal circumstances began intertwining with my academic journey. Challenges emerged like ominous storm clouds, threatening to dampen my aspirations.

When I stepped onto the campus grounds, I faced an overwhelming workload that seemed impossible to conquer. From mathematical equations that danced before my eyes to complex scientific theories that swirled in my mind like a never-ending labyrinth, it felt as if the very essence of academia was conspiring against me.

I was not one to back down easily. I summoned my inner strength with every obstacle and pressed forward. I sought solace in the vast halls of knowledge, tirelessly seeking guidance from my professors and mentors. Their wisdom, like flickers of a distant light in a dark tunnel, showed me enlightenment.

However, just as I began to feel a glimmer of hope that my academic journey would find its rhythm, personal issues arrived uninvited to fuel the fire. As I trudged through my coursework, I carried the weight on my shoulders on how I could escape from this nightmare.

Yet, within the depths of despair and turbulence, I discovered an unwavering faith in the grace of God. I believed that God guided my steps through every trial and tribulation. I found comfort and solace in the knowledge that I was never alone. Even when life seemed overwhelming, I trusted that there was a divine plan unfolding before my eyes.

However, my encounters did not end there. During one of my weeks of school at the campus, I stumbled upon Michael, a familiar face from my congregation. Michael's warm smile and contagious enthusiasm made him an instant friend. United by their shared faith and love for their community, Michael and I spent countless hours volunteering and doing other activities in our free hours, working on-campus activities, and spreading joy wherever we went.

Amidst this vibrant tapestry of friendships, I couldn't help but be overjoyed when I crossed paths with Patience, an old high school classmate and dear friend. Our reunion was filled with laughter and nostalgic memories of our younger years. Together, we navigated the challenges of college life, supporting each other through thick and thin. Patience's unwavering loyalty reminded me of the importance of true friendship and its power to overcome any obstacle.

As time passed, I continued to be amazed by the diverse and extraordinary individuals I encountered at Borough of Manhattan Community College. Among the sea of students, I discovered many talents, dreams, and stories waiting to be unfolded. The vibrant personalities, innovative thinkers, and passionate souls I met enriched my journey, expanding her horizons and opening my eyes to the beautiful tapestry of human diversity.

Each day at college, I brought new adventures and opportunities for growth. My encounters with Huang, who had become a friend at heart; Sekou, my academic mentor; Michael, the beacon of joy; and Patience, a young lady who never ran out of interesting topics to discuss, there were times I thought in my head, maybe she could become a news anchor a journalist, she was good at coming up with interest topics. We formed an unbreakable bond, sharing dreams, laughter, tears, and triumphs.

Reflecting upon my time at Borough of Manhattan Community College, I am grateful for the extraordinary people who crossed my path. They had not only shaped my college experience but had left an indelible mark on my journey through life. Huang, Sekou, Michael, Patience,

Biwei, and the countless other remarkable students I've met along the way have each contributed a unique walk to the tapestry of my personal story.

***

As a Borough of Manhattan Community College (BMCC) student, I participated in many extracurricular activities on and off campus. These activities allowed me to expand my knowledge and skills and provided numerous opportunities to engage with individuals from diverse backgrounds and work towards addressing critical global issues.

One of the organizations I was proudly associated with was UNICEF. As a member, I participated in various initiatives to improve children's lives worldwide. Whether organizing fundraising events or volunteering my time at local schools, being part of UNICEF ignited my passion for advocating for the rights and well-being of vulnerable children.

In addition to my involvement with The United Nations International Children's Emergency Fund (UNICEF), I also dedicated my time and energy to the United Nations Association of United States of America (UNA-USA). This organization allowed me to deeply understand the United Nations and its work in promoting peace, human rights, and sustainable development. Attending conferences and engaging in thought-provoking discussions further nurtured my interest in international affairs and global governance.

AMID MY QUESTIONABLE EXISTENCE

One of my most transformative experiences during college was being selected as a Youth Delegate at the Friendship Ambassadors Foundation. This role allowed me to represent my community and engage in cultural exchanges with young people worldwide. Together, we fostered greater cross-cultural understanding and addressed issues such as climate change, poverty, and education.

Moreover, as a Student Activity participant at the New York Public Interest Research Group (NYPIRG), I actively engaged in campaigns and projects related to social and environmental justice. Whether advocating for affordable education or promoting sustainable practices on our campus, my involvement in NYPIRG allowed me to develop leadership skills and make a tangible impact within my community.

All these extracurricular activities shaped me into a more well-rounded individual and provided invaluable experiences. Through my involvement, I learned to collaborate with people from diverse backgrounds, think critically about complex issues, and take the initiative to address them.

My time at BMCC was not confined to the classroom walls. Instead, it served as a stepping stone for my engagement in various extracurricular activities that broadened my horizons and helped me develop as a leader. United Nations International Children's Emergency Fund (UNICEF), I also dedicated my time and energy to the United Nations

Association of United States of America (UNA-USA) to Friendship Ambassadors Foundation (FAF) and NYPIRG; each organization contributed to my growth and allowed me to establish meaningful connections with individuals equally passionate about creating positive change in the world.

Following the year 2019, after moving to a new neighborhood, I remember it was the scorching summer when my dad made the fateful decision to abandon his own family, leaving behind my mom, my two sisters, and me. It was a heart-wrenching scene, witnessing the departure of my father, whom I had known and cherished since the moment I entered this world. The betrayal and heartache I felt were immeasurable, and I couldn't fathom how someone in their right mind could so callously tear apart a family.

The days that followed were filled with endless questioning and soul-searching. How could I ever find it within myself to forgive someone who could inflict such pain? Though the wounds were raw and profound, I realized that ignoring him was not an act of absolution for him but rather a means for me to let go of the resentment holding me back. However, I resolved that forgiveness did not equate to deserving my respect.

Amid turmoil and turmoil, I came to a stark realization. Life would go on despite the shattered foundation of our family. As heartbroken as I was, I knew I had to gather my broken pieces and stay focused on my academic journey. With unwavering determination, I threw myself into my studies—immersing myself in books, exploring new concepts, and aiming for excellence in every endeavor.

The academic realm became my refuge, a sanctuary for my troubled heart. I would navigate through equations daily, analyze literature, and stretch my intellectual limits. The challenges of complex problem-solving and critical analysis provided a much-needed distraction from the tumultuous emotions swirling within me.

As time passed, my dedication bore fruit. The trials of my personal life did not define my academic performance; instead, they fueled a fierce hunger for success. With each passing exam, assignment, or project, I realized that my resilience was something to be proud of. I had surpassed the boundaries set by my circumstances, proving that I was more than just a victim of an unfortunate incident.

The support system that enveloped me during this trying time was also instrumental in my healing process. My mother, despite her pain, became my guiding light, offering unwavering love and encouragement. My sisters, who shared in my despair, strengthened our bond as we leaned on each other for support. Together, we formed an unbreakable unity, picking up the pieces left behind by our absent father.

As the years passed, I understood that the betrayal I experienced did not define me; it was merely a chapter in my story. Life had bestowed upon me both triumphs and tribulations, and the weight of my father's abandonment became a catalyst for personal growth and perseverance.

Looking back on that summer of 2019, I can now reflect upon the strength I summoned during those dark days. Through the power of forgiveness, resilience, and an unyielding focus on my academic pursuits, I found solace and constructed a foundation for a brighter future.

Today, as I stand proud in adversity, I am grateful for the lessons learned and the journey traveled. The scars of that heartbreaking summer remind me of my endurance—a testament to my indomitable spirit. As I forge ahead on my path toward success, I embrace the knowledge that I can overcome any challenge that comes my way.

***

In the depths of my heart, I found the strength to move on from the profound pain of my father's abandonment. It was a difficult journey, filled with countless obstacles that tested my resilience and determination. Despite the avalanche of emotions threatening to drown me, I solemnly vowed to rise above the turmoil and forge my path.

As I stepped into the labyrinth of my academic year, I encountered a series of ups and downs. Life seemed determined to challenge me at every corner, presenting setback after setback to hinder my progress. The weight of failure loomed large, threatening to cast its piercing shadow over my aspirations.

Classes became a battlefield where I fought tirelessly, armed with an unwavering determination to conquer the challenges. Yet, time and again, it felt like victory slipped through my fingers like desert sand. My dreams teetered on the edge of extinction, and doubts began to gnaw at my spirit.

I dropped out of classes to shield myself from the pain of repeated failure. It seemed like the only option when the storm of despair threatened to consume me whole. Each withdrawal felt like a dagger piercing my pride, for I knew that these actions would place me in grave danger with my college's authorities.

The ominous specter of academic probation loomed ever closer, casting its shadow upon my fragile hopes. I found myself at the precipice of expulsion, staring directly into the abyss of shattered dreams. Yet, hope flickered within me like a stubborn flame in the darkest night.

During this turmoil, I turned my gaze towards the heavens, seeking solace in something greater than myself. Through the grace of God, I found the strength to persevere, to cling onto a sliver of hope when everything appeared lost. In this moment of surrender, I realized surrendering was not an option.

Fueled by newfound determination and resilience forged by challenges, I dedicated myself to the arduous path of redemption. I immersed myself in my studies, laboring ceaselessly to overcome the obstacles that had held me captive for far too long. The pangs of regret, the wounds of disappointment, and the burden of past failures fueled my drive like an inner fire.

Turning to the Academic Committee Standing, I poured my heart and soul into many appeals. I filled page after page with my journey, painting a vivid picture of my transformation and illustrating that my past did not define me. I bared my vulnerabilities, exposing the depths of my struggle in the hope that they would recognize my unwavering resolve to succeed.

Day one turned days into weeks, weeks into months, as I forged ahead with unwavering determination. The rest of the semester became a battlefield where I met each challenge head-on. The sweet fruits of my labor began to materialize, my efforts slowly erasing the stains of failure that once ruined my record.

As I look back on that tumultuous chapter in my life, I am reminded of the strength within us all. Though faced with abandonment and shattered dreams, I refused to succumb to the bitterness and self-pity that threatened to consume me. Instead, I emerged from despair with renewed purpose and an unyielding resolve to shape my destiny.

In the face of adversity, we discover the accurate measure of our character. It is during these moments that our strength shines brightest. We can overcome even the most daunting challenges through grace, perseverance, and an unwavering determination to overcome life's obstacles.

And so, as I continue my journey, I carry with me the scars of past battles as a reminder that through resilience and grit, we can turn adversity into triumph. My story is a testament to the indomitable spirit that rests within us all, an inspiring reminder that we can overcome and achieve greatness no matter our setbacks.

CHAPTER 6

THE YEAR I SURRENDERED MY LIFE TO GOD: TIRED OF LIVING MY WAY

As I continued on my journey as a student in the bustling city of Manhattan, there existed a humble community college called Borough of Manhattan Community College (BMCC) existed. Within its walls, I, an ordinary yet ambitious student, embarked on a journey toward a future filled with possibilities. Little did I know that this path would lead me to unforeseen circumstances and forever alter the course of my life.

AMID MY QUESTIONABLE EXISTENCE

Students from diverse backgrounds gather on a typical day at BMCC to pursue their dreams. As I navigated the sea of knowledge, I was determined to achieve greatness. However, the tides of life had other plans for me.

During one particularly challenging semester, personal woes consumed my every thought. An unexpected event threatened to shatter my focus and derail the dreams I had so painstakingly nurtured. As weeks turned into months, I was enveloped in a cloud of uncertainty and doubt, unable to establish a sense of direction.

Days turned into nights, and nights into solitary contemplation. With every passing hour, the weight of my crisis grew heavier upon my shoulders. It seemed as if the world around me conspired against my aspirations, leaving me bereft of hope. In my despair, I questioned whether anything good could emerge from such a hopeless situation.

But just when all seemed lost, a flicker of resilience ignited. In those moments of darkness, I uncovered an unyielding strength deep within my core. With newfound determination, I made a decision that would forever shape the trajectory of my life. I resolved to embrace the challenges I faced as opportunities for growth and transformation.

With this unwavering resolve, I sought solace in the supportive ecosystem BMCC provided. Professors became guiding lights, illuminating my success path with expert knowledge and compassionate guidance. Peers transformed into allies, offering unwavering support and encouragement as we traversed the arduous terrain together.

As I immersed myself in my studies, I discovered the power of perseverance. Each setback became a stepping stone toward resilience, and every obstacle was an invitation to uncover hidden strengths. Each day, I grew wiser, stronger, and more self-assured.

Not long before, my renewed sense of purpose manifested in tangible achievements. The dark clouds plaguing my life dissipated, replaced by rays of hope and possibility. I surpassed my expectations through dedication and unwavering commitment and became a true scholar.

But it was not just academic success that defined my transformation. The crisis initially threatening to consume me became the catalyst for self-discovery and personal growth. I emerged from the storm stronger, wiser, and with an unyielding belief in my potential.

As I reflect upon this extraordinary journey, I am reminded that life's most profound lessons often arise from the darkest corners of our existence. My turbulent experience at Borough of Manhattan Community College (BMCC) taught me that resilience is not limited to overcoming adversity but encompasses the ability to harness one's circumstances and transform them into opportunities for growth.

And so, dear brothers and sisters, remember this: even in the face of impossible odds, when it seems that nothing good will come of a situation, dig deep within yourself. Unleash your inner strength and embrace the challenges that life presents. Through these very challenges, you will discover the true power that resides within you, forever altering the course of your life for the better.

***

The world awoke to a grim reality on a chilly January morning in 2020. It was a year that would witness immense suffering as a dark cloud of grief and sorrow descended upon every corner of the globe. The year would forever be etched in our memories as a time when humanity confronted an unprecedented challenge – the outbreak of the Coronavirus, or COVID-19.

Anxiety permeated the air as news of this mysterious virus began to circulate. People everywhere were filled with trepidation, unsure of what lay ahead. The virus had originated in Wuhan, China, on that ominous day of December 12, 2019. Little did the world know that it would unleash a wave of devastation and disruption on an unimaginable scale.

Before long, this invisible enemy began its relentless march across continents, infecting people indiscriminately. No nation or community was spared from its wrath. The World Health Organization declared a global pandemic as governments scrambled to face the rapidly escalating crisis. The world was gripped by fear, uncertainty, and an overwhelming sense of despair.

In the face of this immense challenge, the unity of humanity proved to be our greatest hope. Scientists and researchers worldwide joined forces, working tirelessly to unlock the secrets surrounding COVID-19. In laboratories and medical facilities, these dedicated individuals battled day and night, their collective resolve unyielding in their quest for a solution. The urgency of the situation instilled an unprecedented sense of purpose within them.

Meanwhile, governments and institutions mobilized all available resources to combat the virus and protect their citizens. Economies stopped, schools shuttered their doors, and public spaces fell eerily silent. An unsettling hush replaced the cacophony of bustling streets and jubilant laughter – the world seemed suspended in time.

Alarmingly, healthcare systems were stretched to their limits as doctors and nurses bravely confronted the onslaught of patients flooding hospitals. These valiant healthcare workers became the unsung heroes of this gripping tale, putting their lives on the line to protect ours. Their unwavering dedication and selflessness became a beacon of hope in these dark times.

In the face of unparalleled adversity, acts of kindness and solidarity emerged as vital threads binding our global community together. Neighbors checked in on each other, offering support and a listening ear. Communities rallied together to provide aid and sustenance to the vulnerable, ensuring no one was left behind.

Amidst the darkness, small glimmers of hope began to emerge. Scientists across the globe raced to develop vaccines and implement effective testing protocols. Their tireless efforts bore fruit as, one by one, vaccines were authorized and rolled out to a weary world. Hearts fluttered with newfound optimism as needles pierced skin, delivering a dose of hope and a chance at liberation from the clutches of the virus.

As we navigated this despair labyrinth, we discovered resilience and strength reservoirs within ourselves. Families reunited over Zoom calls, finding solace in each other's virtual presence. Creativity flourished as artists turned to their crafts to process their emotions and provide relief to others. Our shared human experience, while marred by sorrow, forged bonds that would forever define us.

On this tumultuous journey, the resilience of the human spirit shone through. We picked up the fragments of our shattered lives, one shard at a time, and began rebuilding with determination and grit. The lessons learned during this crisis would forever alter our perception of the world, emphasizing the importance of vulnerability, compassion, and collective action.

And so, as the year ended, we breathed a sigh of relief, bidding farewell to the dark shadows that had plagued us for so long. The year 2020 has been a tale of immense hardship and loss, but it has also been a testament to the strength and resilience of humanity. We emerged scarred yet resilient, ready to face the challenges that lay beyond the horizon with newfound wisdom and compassion.

As we entered a new year, a flicker of hope ignited. We had weathered the storm together and would welcome the dawn of a brighter future.

***

During the tumultuous year of 2020, nations were confronted with an unprecedented crisis that shook the very foundation of their existence. As the menacing virus known as COVID-19 began its relentless spread across the globe, governments were forced to make difficult decisions to safeguard their citizens.

In a joint effort to protect their beloved populations, these nations made an extraordinary proclamation—they declared a nationwide lockdown. With heavy hearts, they announced the shuttering of schools and universities, leaving the corridors of education eerily silent, the vibrant energy of youthful minds confined to the four walls of their homes.

As the world adjusted to this new reality, the whispers of uncertainty began to echo through every household. Students, educators, and parents alike were left grappling with navigating the challenges of this unexpected turn of events. But amidst the chaos and confusion, a glimmer of hope emerged—a lifeline that promised to bridge the physical gap while preserving the sanctity of education. This newfound beacon of knowledge was none other than virtual interaction.

With a deep breath and a longing for continuity, schools, and universities, they embarked on a journey into uncharted territory. Through the power of technology, students assembled in virtual classrooms where they were greeted by the familiar faces of their teachers, who had valiantly adapted their teaching methods to suit this digital landscape. The static hum of computer screens replaced the lively chatter of students exchanging ideas, but a sense of camaraderie prevailed despite physical separation.

In this virtual realm, desks became pixels, whiteboards turned digital, and the click-clack of keyboard strokes echoed throughout countless homes. Dedicated educators took it upon themselves to ensure no student was left behind in this brave new educational frontier. Hours were spent fine-tuning lesson plans and refining online resources, all to preserve the sanctity of learning.

Parents also played their part, transforming living rooms and kitchens into impromptu classrooms. Daily routines were disrupted but adapted, as the familiar structure of a traditional school day was molded to fit within the parameters of virtual education. Gone were the morning school runs and hurried lunches, replaced by parents who stepped into the dual role of caregiver and facilitator, guiding their children through this uncharted territory.

Yet, amid the chaos, a silver lining emerged. The virtual realm offered a unique opportunity for students and educators to discover new avenues of creativity and connection. Peer collaboration harnessed the power of technology as aspiring writers crafted masterpieces through collaborative virtual storytelling sessions. Budding scientists conducted experiments from the comfort of their own homes, their virtual laboratories brimming with a sense of wonder and discovery.

For every obstacle that was encountered, an innovative solution was found. Field trips became digital excursions, with students exploring the world behind their computer screens. The wonders of ancient civilizations materialized through virtual museum tours, and guest speakers from all corners of the globe brought expertise to these eager minds through video conferencing.

Though the physical barriers persisted, virtual interaction paved the way for resilience and adaptability. It sparked an unforeseen revolution as teachers and students discovered hidden talents, unwavering determination, and a sense of community transcending distance.

As with any tale worth telling, this story had its fair share of challenges. Technological glitches attempted to disrupt the learning rhythm, internet connections waxed and waned, and the occasional out-of-sync audio dampened spirits. However, the strength of human nature proved unmatched, as perseverance overcame every obstacle thrown in its path.

In that fateful year of 2020, both nations emerged from lockdown, their citizens reminiscent of battle-worn warriors. They carried within them the collective knowledge gained from a year of virtual education, forever transformed by the challenges they had triumphed over together. And though the scars of this unprecedented time would forever be etched in their memories, so too would the triumphs and immeasurable growth celebrated during these virtual interactions.

The nation's leaders recognized the enduring value of the virtual realm, and thus, it continued to be woven into the fabric of education even as physical classrooms reopened. The hallowed halls of learning were forever changed, with virtual interaction standing firmly alongside traditional methods, forging a new path that 2020 had so unexpectedly illuminated.

And so, the tale of 2020 and its profound impact on education ended, leaving future generations with a legacy to behold. A testament to the indomitable human spirit, the story of virtual interaction and its role in navigating these turbulent times would be recounted for years to come—a story of resilience, imagination, and the ability to connect beyond borders together.

Amid a worldwide quarantine, I embarked on a new academic year. The educational landscape had significantly transformed, presenting me with unforeseen challenges. As a student passionate about excelling in my studies and staying ahead of the curve, I knew I had to adapt to this new reality of remote learning and redefine how I interacted with my classes.

Stepping into this unfamiliar territory, I realized that the physical walls of the classroom had been replaced with virtual spaces. Gone were the energetic discussions that echoed through the hallways, and instead, a quiet hush settled over our digital platforms. It was as if the world had entered a frozen state, yet I was determined to continue my journey towards academic excellence.

As the days melted into weeks, I navigated through this new way of class interaction, eager to stay on top of my classwork and maintain a well-organized schedule. Adapting required a sense of resilience and an unwavering commitment to learning. It meant embracing technology as my gateway to education, allowing it to bridge the gap between me and my professors, classmates, and educational resources.

Each week, I participated in virtual lectures, engaging in online discussions, and submitting assignments as digital uploads. Despite the absence of face-to-face interactions and the palpable silence that greeted me through the screen, I refused to let myself succumb to complacency. I resolved to forge meaningful connections with my professors and fellow students, even if it meant doing so virtually.

As I moved forward with my academic year, there were times when I had to adapt to a new way of class interaction to be on top of my class work and schedule while the rest of the world was still in quarantine.

In this time of isolation and uncertainty, I discovered a remarkable strength within myself—a determination that refused to waver. My classmates and I became virtual comrades, seeking solace and reassurance on this unfamiliar journey. Together, we embraced these uncharted waters, offering support and encouragement through messages and video calls.

As the world grappled with the pandemic that held it captive, I realized that, despite the physical distance that separated us, we were bound by a shared goal: to emerge triumphant from the realm of academia. This global crisis catalyzed innovation, challenging me to find creative ways to thrive in an environment that demanded adaptability.

Gone were the days of rushing between lectures and juggling extracurricular activities, but my passion for learning remained resolute. Each day, I immersed myself in the virtual realm of knowledge, utilizing every available resource to enhance my understanding and expand my intellectual horizons.

Although I had yearned for the traditional hustle and bustle of student life, this extraordinary circumstance taught me invaluable lessons about flexibility, adaptability, and resilience. It revealed that physical boundaries need not limit our capacity for growth and accomplishment. With every virtual interaction, I discovered that the spirit of learning could permeate through screens and transcend the confines of isolation.

And so, as the academic year progressed, I embraced the new standard and excelled within it. Through sheer determination and a hunger for knowledge, I surpassed my expectations. This journey taught me that success is not solely measured by grades but rather by our ability to adapt, innovate, and persevere in adversity.

In the end, as I reflect upon this transformative experience, I realize that I discovered newfound capabilities within myself during times of hardship. I emerged from this academic year stronger and confident in my ability to navigate any challenges that lie ahead. The world may have remained in a state of quarantine. Still, I emerged triumphant within academia—a testament to the power of the human spirit and its unwavering pursuit of education, even amidst the most trying circumstances.

***

In the same year, 2020, life seemed to unfold in a manner none could have fathomed. In a time filled with uncertainty and chaos, a peculiar awakening occurred within the depths of my soul. Little did I know, this was the year that would forever alter the trajectory of my existence, compelling me to surrender my life to God.

Looking back, it becomes vividly clear how wearied I had become by living according to my whims and desires. The constant pursuit of worldly pleasures had left me hollow and unfulfilled. Deep within, a yearning for something greater, something transcendent, germinated, softly beckoning me towards a higher purpose.

Perhaps the quiet solitude of isolation or the whispers of an unseen hand guiding me amid turbulence led me to question my life's direction. As the world faced unprecedented trials, I learned that a divine plan exists, a purpose greater than our mortal comprehension.

During one sad night, as darkness enveloped my surroundings, I gazed into the starry tapestry adorning the heavens. With each gleaming star casting its unique brilliance upon the canvas of eternity, I felt awe and wonder. In that moment, I surrendered my pride, fears, and doubts to the hands of a Creator beyond human grasp.

From that point on, my journey steered towards a path unlike any I had traversed previously. No longer was I solely concerned with my ambitions; now, I sought to align my footsteps with the cosmic plan designed specifically for me. It was as if the veils of illusion lifted, revealing a tapestry woven intricately with each choice and each event that had led me to this pivotal moment.

Every step became a testament to my newfound dedication to seeking and living according to God's will. The pursuits that once consumed my life now seemed insignificant against the backdrop of divinity. Riches, power, and indulgences faded compared to the purity and fulfillment of following the guiding light of a compassionate and omniscient force.

With each passing day, I became more attuned to the rhythms of life outside of my narrow existence. Deep within my heart, I discovered the hidden treasure of empathy, compassion, and unconditional love. I no longer viewed the world through selfish lenses but rather through the eyes of a humble servant seeking to embody the divine qualities bestowed upon humankind.

Through this surrender, my purpose became clear. No longer was I a mere passenger on the sea of existence, aimlessly adrift. I had become a co-creator, an instrument through which God's love and wisdom could be channeled to impact the lives of others. Each interaction, each encounter presented an opportunity to sow seeds of kindness, to offer a listening ear or a helping hand.

Thus, 2020 marked a profound turning point in my life – a year that witnessed the ignition of hope amidst despair and the dawning of faith amidst doubt. No longer did I confine myself within the boundaries of my ambitions; instead, I entrusted my life to the will of God, allowing divine providence to chart the course ahead.

I wish you to embark on your odyssey through the story of life; you, too, find the courage to surrender your desires, fears, and doubts to the infinite wisdom that resides in the embrace of God's will. It is within this surrender that true liberation is found, and the seedlings of a purposeful existence take root and blossom into a beautiful tapestry of divine guidance and love.

Moving forward, I remember sitting on the edge of my bed, contemplating the events that had unfolded in my life since the remarkable year of 2020. It was a year of immense significance for me, as it marked the beginning of a journey that would shape my future and bring me closer to my faith.

In that fateful year, I experienced a series of vivid dreams that left an indelible mark on my soul. I dreamt of ascending to the sky three nights between May and July. Each plan was remarkably similar yet distinct in its own way. My celestial journey seemed prophetic, hinting at an unknown destiny waiting for me.

Curiosity and spiritual yearning consumed my thoughts, prompting me to seek solace in prayer one night. Stirred by longing, I rose from my slumber at 3 am and kneeled to converse with God. As the words escaped my lips, I fervently surrendered my life and all-encompassing it to the divine presence above.

From that moment on, I noticed subtle shifts in my life. A season of isolation has gripped my spirit, compelling me to examine the depths of my soul in search of a higher purpose. Days turned into weeks and weeks into months as I delved within myself to unravel the hidden mysteries.

One sunny afternoon, as I went about my daily routine, my mother beckoned me into the sanctuary of her room. With a soft yet assured voice, my mother spoke words that would forever resonate within my heart.

"Rachel, my daughter," my mother began, a glimmer of preternatural wisdom twinkling in her eyes. "I see there's something extraordinary that God has in store for your life."

Perplexed by this cryptic statement, my mind buzzed with questions. But before I could voice my uncertainties, my mother gently admonished me to trust and believe without question. These words of unwavering faith stirred Rachel's spirit, planting seeds of trust within her soul.

As I stood before my mother, uncertainty giving way to surrender, I felt a weighty hand land upon my head. In this moment of humility and devotion, my mother dedicated me to God, consecrating me to a path delicately laid out by unseen forces.

Days turned to weeks as I began to gain a deeper understanding of my purpose and destiny. The dots slowly connected, forming a tapestry of meaning and significance in my life. The dreams, prayers, and moments of isolation all started the intricate threads of a divine masterpiece.

And so, I embarked on a lifelong journey of faith and purpose. I embraced them with an open heart, no longer bewildered by my mother's prophetic words. The dedication bestowed upon me had set me on a path where I would intertwine my desires with the divine will.

Years have passed since that significant year of decision, yet I still carry the weight of that dedication within her heart. Guided by the wisdom of dreams and the enthusiasm of prayer, I stride forward with unwavering faith, ready to embrace whatever wonders and challenges lie ahead on my sacred journey.

After a couple of months, I surrendered my life to God. I found myself at a crossroads. It all began after my mother's dedication to ensuring my well-being and spiritual growth. Little did I know that commitment would soon set me on a path that would test my strength, faith, and resilience like never before.

As the world's weight seemed to settle heavily upon my shoulders, I knew in my heart that it was time for deep spiritual warfare. I embarked on intense prayer and fasting, seeking solace and guidance from above. And during these sacred moments, God started to reveal the things I needed to break free from in my life.

One by one, God began to remove the shackles of family generational curses that had unknowingly hindered my progress. Through divine intervention, He helped me discard old habits that had held me back and distanced me from His ultimate plan for my life. Moreover, He orchestrated the removal of specific individuals who were not aligned with His purpose for me, clearing the path for growth and transformation.

This journey was undoubtedly one filled with loneliness. Although physically surrounded by my family, I felt an overwhelming void. Nights spent in prayer and contemplation have often left me feeling isolated, day by day. The burdens of this inner struggle started taking their toll, leading me down the treacherous path of depression. Furthermore, my academic life suffered as I found it increasingly difficult to stay on top of my studies, almost pushing me towards quitting school altogether.

But even in my darkest moments, it was the encouraging words of my mother that reminded me of the strength I possessed within. Her unwavering support and love provided the foundation upon which I could build my resolve and fight against the challenges that threatened to consume me. From the depths of my soul, I whispered a heartfelt "thank you" to my beloved mother for being my anchor in the storm.

Amid this profound solitude, I learned to rely on God and God alone. Through Him, I found solace, strength, and unwavering guidance.

God began to dispatch signs and confirmations in His infinite wisdom, aligning perfectly with the challenges I faced at just the right moments. Motivational videos, thought-provoking sermons, and even biblical revelations converged to bolster my faith and reassure me that I was not alone.

And just as the winds of change swept over me, I realized this was only the beginning. The revelations and breakthroughs of this spiritual journey were merely the first few steps on a much more profound and purposeful voyage. The challenges I faced, the battles I fought, and the victories I attained were all part of a divine plan to mold me into the person God intended me to be.

With a committed heart and a steadfast spirit, I embraced the uncertainties ahead. Armed with the knowledge that my heavenly Father had a purpose for my life, I stepped into the next chapter with unwavering faith. The lonely nights and uphill battles were not in vain; they were stepping stones towards a brighter future filled with endless possibilities.

And so, my story continues, intertwined with the tapestry of hope, faith, and redemption. With each passing day, I grow stronger, knowing that God's hand guides every step of this incredible journey. For it is said that in our darkest hours, when we feel most alone, it is then that the light of God shines brightest, leading us out of the darkness and into the radiance of His divine presence.

The heavy weight upon my shoulders has transformed into wings of resilience and determination. With God by my side and my mother's love echoing in my heart, I am ready to face whatever lies ahead. This is just the beginning—a testament to the incredible power of faith, love, and unwavering dedication.

And so, my journey continues, where the pages of my story unfold with every breath I take.

After the dedication from my mother, I started to feel a heavy weight on me. I started a rich spiritual warfare, began to pray, and fast. God started to reveal to me things that I needed to break off my life, which included family generational curses; he began to remove habits and people that were not aligned with His for my life. It was a very lonely journey for me. Even though I was physically together with my family, spiritually. 1 was incredibly lonely. There were times I fell into depression mode, and l also was struggling to stay on top of my classes, which resulted in me almost quitting school altogether. Only my mother's encouraging words made me stronger. Thank you, mommy. The only 1 could rely on was God and Him alone. I began to receive confirmation that aligned with what I was going through right at the perfect time, either through motivational videos, sermons, or Biblical proofs. And This was just the beginning of it all.

A divine realization slowly unfolded as I became aware of what was happening in my life. The Holy Spirit began to reveal the intricacies of my family bloodline, shedding light on the recurring pattern of divorces and separations. It became evident that this issue ran deep, and I resolved to dig deeper to uncover the root cause of this problem.

I approached my mother with a determined heart and earnestly sought her insight. She shared her experiences, providing fragments of the puzzle plaguing our family. Armed with this knowledge, I embarked on a prayer journey, determined to break the generational curses that had haunted us for so long.

I remember inviting my sisters to join me on this arduous path, but they refused. Undeterred, I decided to take on this challenging journey alone. Little did I know the spiritual warfare that awaited me.

The battles I faced were truly indescribable. As I delved further into my prayers, it was as if unseen forces rallied against me. But I pressed on, knowing that this was a battle worth fighting.

Days turned into weeks, weeks into months, as I poured out my heart to God, seeking deliverance for my family. It was not an easy road, but I was fueled by an unwavering faith and a burning desire to see my loved ones set free.

Through the prayers, God revealed deep-rooted wounds and generational patterns needed to be severed. It was a painful process of introspection and repentance as I acknowledged the mistakes and brokenness that flowed through the generations.

Gradually, with each prayer and each surrender, I could sense a shift in the spiritual atmosphere. The chains that had bound my family for so long were beginning to loosen. I could see the grip of generational curses was weakening, giving way to hope and restoration.

Although the journey was solitary, I knew I was not alone. The Holy Spirit provided comfort and strength in moments of doubt and fatigue. It was a partnership between heaven and earth, a divine collaboration in breaking free from the chains of the past.

And then, one by one, I began to understand the secrecy unfolding. From broken relationships, the destructive cycle of divorce and separation started to make sense. The darkness that had plagued my family's bloodline became so clear to me to the point where I had to take action to end it all.

I recognize that my story is but one thread in the tapestry of countless others who have faced their battles. I hope that by sharing my journey, others may find the courage to confront the generational patterns that have hindered their lives.

Overcoming generational curses is not easy, but it is worth pursuing. It is a journey that requires perseverance, faith, obedience to God, and an unwavering belief in the power of prayer. And though the spiritual warfare may be unbelievable, the victory that awaits is immeasurable.

CHAPTER 7

LONGING FOR PEACE AND COMFORT: LETTING GOD TAKE CONTROL OF MY LIFE

Longing for God's comfort and peace has always been the driving force in my life. From a young age, I yearned for the presence of God, recognizing that nothing else in this world could genuinely satisfy my heart and desires. With this conviction burning deep within me, I consciously changed everything around me and took my relationship with God seriously.

My journey towards a deeper connection with God started with an unwavering commitment to learn more about Him. I delved into the scriptures, spending countless hours poring over the words of the Bible. In pursuing knowledge, I discovered a wealth of wisdom, comfort, and guidance that strengthened my resolve to draw closer to God.

As I absorbed the teachings within the pages of the Holy Book, I saw glimpses of God's character and immense love for His creation. These revelations sparked a sense of awe, igniting a passion to know Him intimately. I hungered for a personal relationship with the Almighty, a connection that transcended mere knowledge and reached the depths of my soul.

Prayer became my constant companion. I sought solace and guidance in communion with God, pouring out my hopes, fears, and aspirations. In those moments of vulnerability, I found a peace that surpassed all understanding. The weight of the world lifted off my shoulders as I entrusted my cares to the One who holds the universe in His hands.

The path towards a deeper relationship with God was not without its challenges. I encountered doubts, distractions, and moments of weakness. However, my steadfast determination to seek God's presence kept me committed. I knew that the journey would not always be smooth, but the reward of knowing God intimately far outweighed the difficulties along the way.

As my understanding of God expanded, so did my perspective on life. I began to see every situation through faith, understanding that God was working all things together for my good. I discovered a strength and resilience within myself that I never knew existed, guided by the unwavering knowledge that God was by my side every step of the way.

Embracing a life centered on God allowed me to experience His peace during chaos, to find joy in the simplest of moments, and to rest in the knowledge that I was unconditionally loved. My relationship with God became the cornerstone upon which I built my life, guiding every decision, every aspiration, and every interaction.

One truth remained constant through it all - God's love never fails. The more I sought after Him, the more I realized the depths of this love and the more I understood the peace and comfort it brought. Longing for God's presence had propelled me into a life of purpose, meaning, and unending fulfillment.

Reflecting on my journey, I am grateful for the unrelenting longing that led me toward God's comfort and peace. Through this pursuit, I have discovered my true purpose in life, and it is through this pursuit that I continue to find solace and guidance in every season. The depth of God's love is immeasurable, and I am forever humbled to be a recipient of His grace.

As I waited for one more semester to come by, excitement coursed through my veins as I eagerly anticipated receiving emails from the prestigious Borough of Manhattan Community College (BMCC). These emails would contain vital information regarding the graduation process. The tangible realization of my hard work and dedication was finally within reach.

Unable to contain my delight, I bounded towards the campus, eagerly readying myself for a memorable graduation photo shoot. As I arrived, anticipation permeated the air, as if the atmosphere knew that dreams would be fulfilled.

To my delight, a package had arrived for me in the mail. I carefully unwrapped it, revealing my pristine graduation gown. Its fabric shimmered under the light, mirroring the gleam in my eyes. Holding it gently, I couldn't help but imagine myself donning this academic regalia, basking in the pride and joy accompanying this momentous occasion. Days turned into hours and minutes as I counted down to the official commencement ceremony.

AMID MY QUESTIONABLE EXISTENCE

In the early year of 2021, my journey as a student at Borough of Manhattan Community College was reaching its end. It was a time filled with mixed emotions as I eagerly awaited the dawn of a new chapter in my life. And so, as I completed my last semester at Borough of Manhattan Community College and embarked on new adventures, she carried the cherished memories, life lessons, and profound friendships she forged along the way. Their stories will forever remain woven into the fabric of Rachel's existence, reminding us that our lives are composed of the people we meet and the connections we cultivate.

At Borough of Manhattan Community College, I met some of the most outstanding students, including Huang, a former classmate whom I met for the first time in the 2018 summer semester from Professor Havercome, who taught English. Sekou was my peer mentor for half a year; Michael, a known person from church; Patience, my high school classmate and friend; and other outstanding students.

On a scorching summer day in June 2021, the sun blazed with vitality as it illuminated the world with its golden radiance. It was a day unlike any other, for on this fateful day, I found myself preparing for the grand event that marked the culmination of years of hard work and dedication – the official commencement at BMCC.

As I settled on the couch, I glanced at the television screen that flickered to life before me. Excitement mingled with nervous anticipation as

I witnessed a mesmerizing display of names seamlessly sliding across the screen. Each character reminded me of countless struggles overcome, sleepless nights studying, and friendships forged throughout my educational journey.

The weight of the past year's challenges hung in the air as memories of quarantine and isolation floated through my mind. The pandemic had cast its long, dark shadow over our lives, disrupting our routines and altering the course of our journeys. In the face of adversity, resilience and adaptability have become our allies.

As I gazed at those scrolling names, I couldn't help but reflect on the remarkable memories in my heart forever. The resiliency of the human spirit revealed itself in the face of unexpected challenges. Despite the isolation that engulfed us, technology had become a beacon of hope, connecting us virtually and bridging the physical distances.

From attending classes through virtual platforms to joining study groups via video conferencing, our determination knew no bounds. Our bond as distant souls united by a common goal was unbreakable. We celebrated victories and consoled each other during moments of despair, virtually sharing the weight of our academic burdens.

The lessons learned during quarantine were invaluable. It taught us patience, fortitude, and the power of human connection, even from a distance. We discovered that the beauty of learning transcends the traditional confines of a classroom, reaching far beyond the limitations we once knew.

As I continued to watch those names slide across the screen, I couldn't help but feel immense gratitude for the support and guidance I received from my professors and mentors. They had been our guiding lights during these tumultuous times, always ready to lend a listening ear or an encouraging word.

But now, as the day of our official commencement dawned upon us, a sense of pride swelled within me. We were no longer just names flashing across a screen; we were warriors who had emerged victorious in uncertainty. We had proven that no obstacle was insurmountable and no dream too distant.

Summer rays filtered through the windows, painting the room in hues of warmth and promise. With a firm resolve, I glanced at the names cascading down the screen, etching them deeply within my memory. The time had come to bid farewell to this chapter of my life and eagerly embrace the next.

As I rose from the couch, ready to embark on this momentous day, I carried the lessons learned during quarantine, the friendships formed against all odds, and the unyielding determination to chase my dreams. The official commencement at BMCC would forever testify to our indomitable spirits and unwavering pursuit of knowledge.

With a heart filled with gratitude, I made my way toward the door, leaving behind the comfort of that couch and stepping into a world brimming with possibility. The summer of 2021 had marked not the end but rather the beginning of a new chapter, where we would transform our dreams into reality, guided by the memories and experiences we would never forget.

The illustrious Borough of Manhattan Community College (BMCC) stood within the bustling streets of a vibrant city. And in the heart of this thriving institution, a remarkable journey unfolded, woven with threads of faith, determination, and grace.

Reflecting on the bountiful moments and challenges I encountered at BMCC, my heart swells with gratefulness that words cannot fully capture. Graduating from this esteemed institution taught me invaluable lessons about the extraordinary power within each of us.

With unwavering determination, I embarked on my academic path, convinced that dreams can be transformed into reality. As the sun cast warm rays upon the hallowed hallways of BMCC, I sought solace in knowing that God's grace guided my footsteps. In every lecture, discussion, and assignment, I witnessed the undeniable force of a higher power nudging me toward greatness.

No obstacle could deter me from pursuing my dreams, for I understood that resilience and a steadfast belief in one's abilities would triumph over any adversity. The challenges presented along the way were merely stepping stones, paving the path toward my destination.

In embracing BMCC's diverse community, I found strength through the shared tales of countless individuals who had conquered their mountains. Their stories were akin to a symphony of perseverance, each note harmonizing with mine. We created a mighty chorus celebrating the human spirit and the indomitable will to succeed.

As I delved deeper into my studies, I discovered that education was not confined to the four walls of a classroom. Beyond textbooks and exams, BMCC became a sanctuary where intellectual growth thrived. Fueled by an unquenchable thirst for knowledge, I dared to question the norms and explore new horizons.

AMID MY QUESTIONABLE EXISTENCE

Like guiding beacons in an uncharted sea, the professors rendered unwavering support and nurtured my thirst for learning. Their expertise and passion stirred my curiosity, fueling a flame within me that burned brighter with each passing day. They instilled in me the belief that greatness resided within my grasp, awaiting only my recognition.

BMCC's vibrant tapestry transcended the confines of education. Within its lively student organizations, I discovered companions who shared my aspirations and walked alongside me as we wove our dreams into reality. Together, we danced to the rhythm of creativity, camaraderie, and collaboration, leaving an indelible mark on the canvas of our lives.

AMID MY QUESTIONABLE EXISTENCE

My graduation from Borough of Manhattan Community College was a certificate of achievement and a testament to the transformative power of perseverance and faith. It stood as a beacon of hope, reminding all who witnessed my arduous journey that miracles were not just the terrain of legends but gifts bestowed upon even the humblest of individuals.

With gratitude in my heart and newfound wings of knowledge, I took flight from the hallowed grounds of BMCC into a world brimming with endless possibilities. The indomitable spirit fostered within me during my remarkable journey carried me forward, propelling me toward success while colored by the brushstrokes of faith, determination, and grace.

AMID MY QUESTIONABLE EXISTENCE

Reflecting upon those cherished years at Borough of Manhattan Community College (BMCC), I do so with a profound sense of fulfillment. For my journey, there was not merely an accumulation of degrees or accolades but a deep experience that shaped my mind and soul.

So, fellow dreamers and seekers of greatness, let us remember that with God's grace, unwavering determination, and unyielding faith, no obstacle could stand in the way of our dreams. May we chart our remarkable journeys, embracing the transformative power of perseverance and grace, for who knows what wondrous miracles await those who dare to believe?

After a few months of graduating from BMCC, I took a well-deserved break from the hustle and bustle of academic life. As the days turned into weeks and months, I found solace in the comfort of my home, allowing myself time to reflect on the journey that had brought me here and the path ahead.

Within the confines of my humble abode, I delved deep into contemplation, pondering the possibilities that awaited me soon. The decisions I needed to make loomed large in my mind, shimmering with excitement and trepidation. At this juncture, I realized the pivotal role my career choice would play in shaping my destiny.

During those moments of introspection, when the world seemed to fade away, I yearned to find a sign - a divine indication of the path that God intended for me. Would I discover success through medicine, or perhaps I was meant to unearth the mysteries of science? The possibilities were endless, and yet, the answer eluded me.

Days turned into nights as I sought guidance from the heavens above. My heart whispered fervently, praying for clarity and direction in this crucial phase of my life. As I stared at the twinkling stars each night, I wondered if they held the key to my future. It was as if the cosmos conspired to guide me toward my true calling.

One fine evening, just as the sun began its descent, painting the sky with hues of gold and crimson, an unexpected visitor arrived at my doorstep. A wise older man, his face etched with timeless wisdom and eyes filled with compassion, stood before me. It was like an embodiment of divine guidance had appeared at my doorstep.

Curiosity mingled with awe as he handed me a small, weathered book – a relic of ancient knowledge passed down through generations. In hushed tones, he revealed that this was no ordinary book; it contained stories of extraordinary individuals who had embarked on journeys like mine, seeking answers from the divine.

With trembling hands, I opened the book, its pages whispering enchanting tales of hope, courage, and self-discovery. Each narrative resonated deeply within my soul, igniting a fire of inspiration that had laid dormant within me. As I read on, it became clear that the answer I sought was not hidden in a single career choice but rather in pursuing my passions and fulfilling my purpose.

I realized that my skills and talents were not meant to be confined within the boundaries of a single profession. Instead, they were diverse facets of a multifaceted jewel that could shine brightly across various disciplines. The decision awaiting me was not the choice of one path but rather the embracement of a lifelong journey of exploration, growth, and self-discovery.

With newfound clarity, I thanked the wise older man for his timely visit and bid him farewell. After getting accepted by Queens College, I took a break from the Fall 2021 semester until Spring 2022 with an approach, a renewed mind, and determination. I was armed with the ancient wisdom bestowed upon me before I stepped onto the campus grounds, ready to embrace the challenges and opportunities that awaited.

As I looked forward to embarking on my academic journey at Queens College, I vowed to approach each subject with an open mind and a passion for knowledge. No longer bound by the constraints of a predetermined career path, I reveled in the freedom to explore and discover new realms of understanding. I brought fresh insights daily, expanding my horizons and enriching my world knowledge.

I realized that my story continues to unfold with every turn of the page. The future is no longer a daunting abyss but a tapestry waiting to be woven with threads of passion and purpose. Guided by the wisdom I have gleaned, I embrace the uncertainties that lie ahead, secure in the knowledge that my journey shall be filled with infinite opportunities for growth and self-realization.

***

Before the year 2021 comes to an end, I find myself in between a bittersweet mix of excitement and sorrow; I step into the unknown, armed with the love and wisdom inherited from my remarkable Grandpa as I fulfill his immortal wish - never to give up and unconditionally put God first in my life. His words of wisdom have been etched into the depths of my soul, serving as a guiding light in times of darkness. One piece of advice he imparted resonates profoundly: "Never give up and always put God first in your life." These simple yet profound words echo in my mind, reminding me of the strength and faith that guided my grandfather's steps. As I recall all the memories amidst the chaos and uncertainty of the global pandemic, I found solace and comfort in the fond memories of conversations with my beloved Grandpa. He was a strong pillar in my life, but unfortunately, illness had gripped him tightly. The doctors had diagnosed him with cancer, and he had been battling this relentless foe for an extended period.

As I adapted to the new normal of online learning and isolated existence during the quarantine, my heart yearned for human connection and the warmth of familial love. Every afternoon, like clockwork, my dear Grandpa would call me to check on my well-being, offering me his unwavering support and words of wisdom. We created our little sanctuary of love and laughter in these precious moments, spanning the distance between us.

Something was amusing that occurred during our frequent phone calls. I would rush to answer my grandpa's call during my online classes, separated by brief breaks. Without fail, no matter how short the call was, he would always hear my mother's voice informing him that I was in the kitchen. It appears my timing was impeccable as if I were innately drawn there by some invisible force.

Considering this recurring coincidence, my grandpa playfully concocted a nickname for me - "Mama Jiko," which loosely translates to "Mother Kitchen." It was his tender way of humorously acknowledging my constant presence in that culinary domain. From that day forward, I became affectionately known as "Mama Jiko" to him and everyone within our family.

Days turned into weeks and weeks into months, but my grandpa's illness remained relentless. However, despite the despair in our hearts, his cheerful spirit refused to waver. He would call us each day excitedly, eagerly asking about my latest kitchen escapades, joyfully referring to me as "Mama Jiko."

We shared countless stories during those cherished telephone conversations, both mundane and extraordinary. Often, we would explore intriguing recipes and discuss the art of cooking. Despite his physical absence, Grandpa's presence loomed large within our conversations, his voice resonating with love and tenderness.

Then, as fate would have it, the day we had always dreaded arrived. My Grandpa's relentless battle with cancer reached its final chapter. On that fateful day, memories of our phone calls flooded my mind as I sat in the kitchen. I wished with all my heart that I could answer just one more call from him, one more opportunity to hear his voice filled with warmth and affection.

The passing of my dear Grandpa left an immense void in my life. The kitchen that once resonated with his vibrant spirit now seemed incomplete. Yet, amidst the sorrow, I drew strength from the joyous memories we had created together. The nickname "Mama Jiko" symbolized our unwavering bond and a reminder of the love he showered upon me.

Years have passed since then, but my grandpa's presence remains etched in my heart. Each time I step into the kitchen, I can almost hear his voice calling out to me, "Mama Jiko," as if he never left. His legacy lives on through every meal I prepare and every shared moment of laughter in the warmth of family gathered around the table.

Though cancer robbed me of the physical presence of my grandpa, it failed to extinguish the flames of love that danced within my heart. Through the power of memories and the strength of our connection, I find solace and inspiration each day. As I continue my journey in life, I strive to carry forward the legacy of "Mama Jiko" with grace, love, and an unwavering commitment to family.

Looking back, I was still flooded with memories of my grandfather's unwavering dedication and the boundless love he showered upon his family. One could witness a remarkable blend of strength and gentleness in his presence that defined his character. His unparalleled fortitude allowed him to endure the trials and tribulations that life threw his way, never losing sight of what truly mattered - his loved ones.

Grandpa, as I affectionately called him, was never one to preach or sermonize. Yet, his actions spoke louder than any words ever could. He led by example and taught us the true essence of familial love and unity. He instilled the importance of perseverance and resilience in each of us, showing us that we can weather it no matter how fierce the storm.

Standing on the precipice of a new chapter, I carry the weight of continuing Grandpa's legacy. It is not merely a responsibility but an honor. I am determined to embrace the teachings he so graciously bestowed upon me, to embody the love and dedication that defined his existence. In every endeavor, big or small, I strive to emulate the unwavering perseverance that was a cornerstone of my grandfather's character. His tenacity fuels my ambition, his love nourishes my soul, and his wisdom guides my every step. As I continue my journey as a student, I am grateful for the invaluable lessons my grandpa taught me.

Considering this recurring coincidence, my grandpa playfully concocted a nickname for me - "Mama Jiko," which loosely translates to "Mother Kitchen." It was his tender way of humorously acknowledging my constant presence in that culinary domain. From that day forward, I became affectionately known as "Mama Jiko" to him and everyone within our family. Days turned into weeks and weeks into months, but my grandpa's illness remained relentless. However, despite the despair in our hearts, his cheerful spirit refused to waver. He would call us each day excitedly, eagerly asking about my latest kitchen escapades, joyfully referring to me as "Mama Jiko."

***

After two years of surrendering my life to Jesus, I journeyed through various seasons. It became evident that I could sense the changes of season in my spirit and how things operated in the physical realm. However, one of the most significant signs of this transformation was the gradual loss of friendships I cherished.

As I delved deeper into my faith, I encountered heavy spiritual warfare. Forces seemingly opposed to my newfound beliefs began to manifest in my life. I faced setbacks and obstacles that I had never expected. It became increasingly clear that I could no longer cling to the things of my past.

Furthermore, I found myself struggling with financial hardship. Where I once enjoyed relative stability, I now face unexpected difficulties maintaining my economic well-being. These trials served to test both my faith and my obedience to God.

To my dismay, I also experienced persecution from those dearest to my heart. These individuals had previously been a significant part of my life, but now struggled to accept the changes within me. The people I loved and cherished began to view me with suspicion and hatred.

During this difficult season, God challenged me to stand firm in my faith. I sought strength and guidance through prayer and the study of Scripture. Despite the turmoil surrounding me, I clung to the promises of God and found solace in His unwavering love and grace.

Through this period of intense spiritual warfare, setbacks, financial hardship, and the loss of dear friendships, I began to understand the depth of my conviction. My faith, though tested, grew more substantial and more resilient. I discovered a resilience within myself that I had not known existed.

As I navigated these uncharted waters, I realized that my journey with Christ was not meant to be easy. Sacrifices were required, and I had to let go of what held me back. I learned to trust in God's plan for my life, even when it seemed unclear and uncertain.

Looking back, I see these challenges as necessary for my spiritual growth. They refined my character, deepened my faith, and brought me closer to God. Through it all, I understood that life's seasons are not always comfortable or predictable. But by placing my trust in Jesus, I discovered a strength and peace that surpasses all understanding.

Today, I can confidently testify that my trials were not in vain. They shaped me into who I am today and strengthened my relationship with God. The sacrifices made, and the hardships endured were small prices to pay for the immeasurable joy and fulfillment that come from walking faithfully with the Lord.

My journey continues with the certainty that more seasons will come. But armed with the knowledge that God is with me every step of the way, I face the future with unwavering hope and an unshakeable faith.

***

AMID MY QUESTIONABLE EXISTENCE

Looking back on my childhood years, I developed a great appreciation for music. When I was a young girl, I loved listening to music. It was my escape from the troubles of my life. As I listened to the sound of my favorite songs, it felt like my worries were slowly drifting away. Growing up in a tumultuous environment, music acted as a sanctuary, wrapping around me like a warm embrace.

My love for music began innocently enough, with me humming to melodies playing on the radio. I would spend hours mesmerized by the voices of the singers and the way their words conveyed emotions that I couldn't articulate myself. I discovered a language beyond words, deepening my soul through music.

With each passing day, my passion for music grew more assertive. I found solace in the lyrics that mirrored my own experiences and the melodies that carried me to a world far away from my reality. Music became a permanent companion, always there for me, ready to soothe my troubled heart.

In my teenage years, I realized my connection with music ran more profound than mere appreciation. I yearned to be a part of it, to create the same magic that had touched my life in countless ways. I dedicated myself to learning the intricacies of music, exploring different genres, and experimenting with various instruments.

I started taking piano lessons, losing myself in the enchanting melodies the keys under my fingertips produced. The piano became an extension of myself, allowing me to express emotions too complex to be put into words. Through my dedication and relentless practice, I began to excel, winning local competitions and receiving recognition for my talent.

However, my journey with music was challenging. There were moments when self-doubt crept in when I questioned whether I had what it took to pursue my passion professionally. But with the unwavering support of my loved ones and my unyielding desire to make a mark in the music industry, I persisted.

As I embarked on my musical journey, I discovered that music not only had the power to heal the wounds within myself, but it also could touch the lives of others. Whether performing for a crowd, composing a heartfelt melody, or simply sharing my love for music with those around me, I witnessed firsthand the impact that music could have on people's lives.

Music remained a steadfast companion through the ups and downs, the triumphs and failures, guiding me through life's twists and turns. It became more than just an escape; it became a part of my identity. With each note and every chord, I found purpose and fulfillment that surpassed any other pursuit.

Today, as I reflect on my journey, I am grateful for every moment music has given me. It has shaped me into who I am today, teaching me resilience, perseverance, and beauty. I continue to explore the vast realm of music, eager to create my compositions and leave a lasting imprint on those who listen.

AMID MY QUESTIONABLE EXISTENCE

As I look towards the future, I carry the lessons I have learned through my love affair with music. It taught me that even in the face of adversity, a melody is always waiting to be discovered, a harmony yet to be heard. And it is through music that I will continue to navigate the complexities of life, expressing the depths of my soul, one note at a time. As a little girl, music was my escape from the troubles of my life. As I listened to the sound of my favorite songs, it felt like my worries were slowly drifting away.

Every day, when I came home from school, I would sit at my desk and pour my emotions into my notepad. I'd write a mini verse about how my day went and how much I was hurting. Music provided an emotional outlet and a way to express my feelings. It helped me make sense of my emotions and make peace with my inner turmoil.

The music I wrote also provided comfort and peace to other people. Whenever I played my songs for my family and friends, they could feel the emotions I wanted to convey. Music was like a bridge that connected me to the world. It was the light in my dark days and a reminder that everything would be okay.

As the days turned into weeks and the weeks eventually turned into months, I slowly realized that peace, clarity, and comfort were all things that I had to take responsibility for, and they could never be found solely from an outside source. I was the one who had to rely on God for peace and the things that my heart needed the most.

Growing up, I believed that happiness would come from external factors. If I achieved specific goals, possessed certain things, or surrounded myself with the right people, I would automatically find peace and contentment. However, life had a way of showing me that this was not the case.

I faced numerous challenges and disappointments that left me feeling lost and disconnected. My soul was restless, and my heart longed for something more. During this struggle, I began to seek solace in my faith.

Through prayer and introspection, I realized I had been looking in all the wrong places for fulfillment. I had been searching for external validation when the answers were within me. I had to take responsibility for my well-being and find strength in my relationship with God.

I began to cultivate a deeper understanding of myself during this transformative journey. I discovered that true peace and clarity could only be found through self-reflection and surrendering to a higher power. I learned to trust in God's plan and to have faith that everything would work out according to His timing, not mine.

I felt immense comfort as I let go of control and embraced a deeper spiritual connection. Even during life's storms, I knew that I was not alone. There was a sense of peace that surpassed all understanding, giving me the strength to face life's uncertainties.

I discovered a newfound purpose and fulfillment by taking responsibility for my peace and relying on God. I prioritized self-care nourishing my mind, body, and spirit. Reading inspirational books, practicing meditation, and spending time in nature became crucial to my journey towards inner peace.

I also began to surround myself with positive influences, seeking out like-minded individuals who shared the same desire for personal growth and spiritual development. Together, we supported and encouraged one another, creating a community where we could freely express our struggles and celebrate our victories.

Through self-discovery and reliance on God, I gradually transformed my perspective on life. I realized that happiness and fulfillment depended not on external circumstances but on my internal state. I no longer sought validation from others but instead sought assurance from within.

As the days, weeks, and months passed, I experienced a profound shift in my overall well-being. I radiated a sense of peace that attracted positivity into my life. Challenges no longer seemed impossible but rather opportunities for growth and learning. I found comfort in knowing I had the power to create my happiness, regardless of the circumstances.

***

Looking back, I am grateful for the journey that led me to this newfound understanding. My life is a testament to the power of self-reflection, reliance on God, and taking responsibility for one's peace and well-being.

Growing up in a small town, I experienced firsthand the struggles that people faced daily. Poverty was widespread, and opportunities were scarce. The harsh realities of life constantly weighed on my young mind, leaving me feeling lost and hopeless.

But then, I discovered the power of music. It was like a ray of light breaking through the darkness. I found solace in the melodies and lyrics that resonated with my innermost emotions. It became my refuge, my sanctuary in a world that seemed to offer nothing but despair.

I immersed myself in the sounds of various genres, from classical to rock, from jazz to hip-hop. Each artist spoke their truth, their stories intertwined with mine. They became my mentors, guiding me through the complexities of life. Through their music, I learned about love, struggle, and the beauty of the human spirit.

During those tough times, when my family faced financial hardships, and our future seemed uncertain, I would lock myself in my room and lose myself in the melodies. Music gave me an escape, transporting me to a world where dreams were within reach, and hope thrived even in the darkest times.

As I grew older, my love for music deepened. It became a way to cope and a means of self-expression. I began writing my songs, pouring my heart and soul into the lyrics. Music became the language to convey my emotions, fears, and hopes for a brighter tomorrow.

Through music, I found my voice. It gave me the courage to stand up for what I believed in and to fight against the injustices that plagued our society. I realized music could unite people, bridge gaps, and heal wounds.

Reflecting on my journey, I am grateful for music's role in shaping the person I have become. It taught me empathy, resilience, and the power of perseverance. It showed me that even during chaos, there is always a glimmer of hope.

I may not have been able to change the world single-handedly, but music has given me the strength to make a difference in the lives of those around me. I strive to inspire and uplift others through my songs, just as music did for me during my darkest hours.

Music continues to be my constant companion, accompanying me through the highs and lows of life. It is a language that transcends boundaries, touching people's hearts from all walks of life. I am grateful for the gift of music; it has truly saved me and given me a purpose.

As the world around me remains engulfed in chaos, I take solace in the power of music to heal, unite, and bring about change. I am forever indebted to this timeless art form and the artists who have paved the way. Music will forever be my guiding force, my sanctuary amidst the storms of life.

However, I kept the faith. No matter what happened in the world or to me, I never lost faith in God. I turned to prayer to find strength and hope in times of distress. I read the Bible to understand God's plans and promises. I was out for genuine conversations with other believers and volunteers who shared my faith. I always sought ways to spread God's message of love and mercy.

And so, even when the world around me seemed ready to burst into flames, I knew I could still find solace in my faith. I thought of how God was the One who created the world and controlled everything that happened in it. Knowing God was always with me, even during chaos, comforted me. So, I kept faith. I kept believing and trusting that something good would emerge from all the destruction and suffering. Something that would bring confidence back into arenas of confusion and wars. I prayed that the world would one day know God's peace, joy, and love.

No matter how far I traveled – or down whatever dark roads I found myself in – I was always aware of the warmth of God's presence guiding me. I was never alone.

God by my side assured me that I could find something positive in every situation and that I didn't need to fear the future. Whenever I was afraid or overwhelmed by uncertainty, I found strength in knowing that God was with me, just like He had always been.

I was enveloped in a cocoon of familiarity in the vast expanse of my existence. The world around me was a tapestry of routine, where each day mirrored the last, and change was nothing more than a distant and elusive dream.

But little did I know that my life was about to transform as if touched by the divine hands of providence.

It was on an ordinary day, a day like any other, that destiny decided to reveal its magnificent plan. Today, an ethereal force stirred within me, urging me to shed the blinders of complacency and discover the wonders beyond my narrow perception. And it was God, in all His infinite wisdom, who set this grand revelation into motion.

As I embarked upon this journey of enlightenment, I felt a surge of hope amidst a world that seemed unsteady and uncertain. God became the beacon of light illuminating my path, leading me through the labyrinth of doubts and fears. With each step forward, He infused me with a newfound courage, strengthening my resolve to unearth the mysteries that awaited me.

In the depths of my soul, I carried the memories of an ambiguous childhood, where questions lingered like shadows and the past remained shrouded in enigmatic whispers. But with the unwavering presence of the Almighty by my side, those uncertainties transformed into mere remnants of an era long gone. I discovered that it was through Him that I could untangle the knots of my past and rewrite the script for an exhilarating chapter of life yet to come.

Gratitude filled my heart like a cascading waterfall as I recognized the immense power of God's influence in every facet of my being. His omnipresent love ignited a fire, propelling me into unchartered territory with an insatiable thirst for knowledge. Through His divine guidance, I understood the depth of my purpose and limitless potential boundaries.

With every passing moment, I realized there was so much more to learn, so many wonders left to unravel in this vast mosaic called life. Each experience, whether steeped in joy or drenched in sorrow, became a precious lesson intricately woven into the fabric of my existence. Through God's grace, I gained the wisdom to discern the invaluable teachings embedded within every step of my journey.

As I reflected upon the path that had led me here, I couldn't help but feel an overwhelming sense of awe and admiration for the divine orchestrator of my destiny. God had opened my eyes, allowing me to witness the beauty beyond the periphery of my limited perspective. He had given me the courage to embrace change and embark upon a voyage of self-discovery.

In gratitude, I turned my gaze toward the heavens, whispering words of indebtedness to the divine force that had guided me unfailingly. With His unyielding presence, I found solace in uncertainty, strength within vulnerability, and purpose amidst the chaos. My journey was far from over, but with God as my constant companion, I knew I would never walk alone.

And so, with a heart overflowing with gratitude and an insatiable thirst for discovery, I ventured into the unknown, eager to explore the infinite tapestry that lay beyond. I knew that everything I had become, everything I was yet to be, was interwoven with the divine wisdom bestowed upon me by the One who knew me better than I knew myself.

And with each passing day, as I delved deeper into the intricacies of life, I whispered a silent prayer of gratitude, knowing that without God's guiding hand, my life would have remained incomplete. For it was He who had opened my eyes to see the world beyond what I was already used to, and He had set me on a path of discovery that I could have never fathomed on my own.

CHAPTER 8

A NEW PROFOUND MINDSET: SEEING THINGS THROUGH THE LENS OF GOD

Growing up, I was always searching for something more profound. I longed to change the trajectory of my life and gain a new perspective on the world around me. This desire eventually led me to embrace the journey of discovering God's call and purpose for my life.

As a young girl, I found solace in the stories of the Bible. I was captivated by the tales of faith, courage, and redemption that echoed through its pages. These stories opened my eyes to a world beyond my own, where I could be part of a grander narrative.

My understanding of God's plan for my life became more apparent each day. I realized that my purpose was not just to exist but to make a meaningful impact on the lives of others. The biblical perspective allowed me to see that my life had a greater purpose, one that was intricately woven into the fabric of humanity.

As I grew older, I dedicated myself to studying the Word of God. I delved into the scriptures, seeking guidance, inspiration, and answers to my most profound questions. The more I immersed myself in the teachings of the Bible, the more I discovered who I was and what I was meant to do.

God's call for my life became evident as I felt a stirring within my heart. It was a gentle prodding urging me to use my gifts and talents to serve others. I began to understand that my purpose was not some lofty goal to be achieved in isolation but rather a calling to make a tangible difference in the lives of those around me.

With this newfound mindset, I embarked on self-discovery and exploration. I sought opportunities to help those in need, lend a listening ear, and offer a helping hand. I discovered that in giving of myself, I found a sense of fulfillment and purpose that I had never experienced before.

The path was sometimes challenging. There were moments of doubt and uncertainty when I questioned whether I was indeed on the right track. But through it all, I clung to my faith, trusting that God would guide and direct my steps.

Over time, I began to see the impact of my actions. I witnessed lives transformed, hearts healed, and hope restored. In these moments, I realized the true power of embracing God's call and purpose for my life.

Today, as I look back on my journey, I am grateful for the new mindset that I have gained. Through the lens of the Bible, I see the world in a different light. I understand that my life is not just a series of random events but a part of a grander story intricately connected to the divine.

Embracing God's call and purpose for my life has given me a sense of fulfillment and joy that surpasses anything I could have imagined. It has allowed me to make a difference in the lives of others and to be a vessel of God's love and grace.

As I continue this journey, I am excited to see how God will use me in the days ahead. I am ready to embrace the challenges and opportunities that come my way, knowing that with God by my side, I can change the whole story of my life and impact the world around me.

I would wake with hopeful anticipation every day, for I firmly believed that something good would unfold. Despite life's challenges, I balanced my academic and personal pursuits, always striving to nurture a positive mindset.

***

AMID MY QUESTIONABLE EXISTENCE

My journey started during my formative years when I grappled with the pressures of school and the constant whirlwind of personal obligations. It would have been easy to surrender to despair or negativity, but I consciously decided to cultivate my mind and embrace optimism in every situation.

The path I chose was a challenging one. The demands of schoolwork often felt overwhelming, with countless assignments and exams that seemed to be never-ending. However, rather than allowing myself to be consumed by stress, I trained myself to see each challenge as an opportunity for growth. I approached my studies with dedication and a thirst for knowledge, reminding myself that each hurdle I overcame was a stepping stone toward my ambitions.

Outside the realm of academics, I faced a plethora of responsibilities and commitments. There were times when it appeared that the weight of my personal life would compromise my ability to remain positive. Yet, I refused to let the external circumstances define my outlook. Instead, I adopted a proactive approach, seeking ways to integrate personal interests and goals into my daily routine.

During those moments when life seemed particularly burdensome, I developed an unwavering habit of looking up literally and metaphorically. Gazing at the vastness of the world above reminded me that beyond my immediate setbacks and challenges, there existed boundless possibilities. This simple act made me remain hopeful and persevere through the most challenging times.

In the face of adversity, I discovered that positivity was not merely a fleeting emotion but a cultivated mindset that could be honed through conscious effort. I sought inspirational literature, TED talks, YouTube motivational videos, Christian uplifting videos, and motivational podcasts to feed my mind with empowering thoughts and stories of resilience. I surrounded myself with individuals who exuded unwavering optimism, drawing strength from their steadfast belief in the world's goodness.

As the years unfolded, I metamorphosed beyond school and personal life. The positive energy I emanated began to ripple outward, influencing those around me. Friends and acquaintances sought solace in my unwavering positivity, finding support and encouragement in my presence.

My journey through the labyrinth of life has taught me that there is great power in the mind's capacity to cultivate optimism. By embracing positivity as a guiding force, I have transformed challenges into opportunities and setbacks into stepping stones toward personal growth. My path may not always be smooth, but I remain resolute in my commitment to look up to God and see the good, no matter the circumstances.

Reflecting on my life's journey, I am reminded of the many trials and tribulations that have shaped me into who I am today. From humble beginnings, I have learned the importance of resilience, faith, and the power of a positive mindset.

Growing up in a small town, my family faced hardships. My parents worked tirelessly to provide for my siblings and me, but sometimes, we struggled to make ends meet. Despite the challenges, my parents instilled in us the values of hard work, perseverance, and the belief that anything is possible with determination.

Education became my refuge in those early years. I immersed myself in books and knowledge, seeking solace and inspiration. Teaching myself to look beyond the present circumstances, I nurtured a deep faith, trusting that God had a plan for me and that every obstacle was an opportunity for growth.

Upon graduating high school, I faced another hurdle – the financial burden of pursuing higher education. With limited resources, I met the risk of abandoning my dreams. Yet, my unwavering belief in God's providence propelled me forward. I sought scholarships and part-time jobs, determined to acquire the education I desperately desired.

The years that followed were marked by moments of triumph and moments of despair. I experienced setbacks and disappointments, but my faith remained unwavering. During these moments of darkness, I discovered the true strength within me – the resilience to keep pushing forward and the courage to find blessings even during adversity.

As I continued my educational journey, I encountered countless individuals who doubted my abilities and questioned my aspirations. The road to success seemed arduous and riddled with self-doubt. However, I chose not to let their negative words define me. Instead, I clung to my faith, knowing God had planted a seed of greatness within me.

With time, my efforts bore fruit. I graduated with academic achievements, defying the odds stacked against me. At that moment, I fully comprehended the power of a positive mindset and the ability to turn obstacles into stepping stones.

Today, as I reflect upon the chapters of my life, I am grateful for the challenges I have faced. They have molded me into a person of unwavering faith, determination, and compassion. I look back and see God's hand guiding me through the storms, urging me to persevere and reminding me of the good that exists even in the darkest times.

My path may not always be smooth, but I have learned to embrace the journey, knowing that every twist and turn has a purpose. I look up to God, finding the strength to overcome obstacles and the courage to see the good surrounding me.

In sharing my story, I hope to inspire others to never lose sight of their dreams, remain steadfast in their faith, believe in God's power, and live positively. Life may present its challenges, but with determination and an unwavering belief in God's plan, we can overcome anything that comes our way.

As a young girl, I found solace in my faith in God. Facing the challenges and uncertainties of life, I sought refuge in the promise of His love and guidance. I consciously decided to think positively, envisioning my future and the person I aspired to become.

Growing up, I faced various obstacles, both internally and externally. I encountered moments of doubt and fear, but I held on firmly to the belief that my life had a purpose. Holding on to this conviction enabled me to navigate the trials with hope and resilience.

I recognized that life presented me with opportunities for growth and learning. Each setback or disappointment became a steppingstone toward becoming my desired person. Despite the difficulties, I maintained an unwavering faith in God's plan for me.

Throughout my journey, I focused on cultivating gratitude and embracing the present moment. I discovered that I could find joy amidst the challenges by developing an attitude of thankfulness. It allowed me to appreciate the small blessings in life and reminded me of the goodness that surrounded me.

Inspired by faith teachings, I exhibited compassion and kindness toward others. I realized that my journey was not solely about personal growth but also about contributing to the well-being of those around me. Through acts of service and empathy, I sought to make a positive impact on the lives of others, just as God had touched mine.

As I advanced, I encountered success and fulfillment in various aspects. However, I understood that these achievements were not solely the result of my efforts. They were a testament to the faith that shaped my perspective and the support of those who believed in me.

Throughout the years, as I look back, I am grateful for the journey of discovering who I am and the reason for my existence I embarked upon. Embracing my faith has given me a sense of purpose, peace, and hope. It has allowed me to endure the challenges with resilience and persevere through tough times.

I can testify to the transformative power of faith and the ability to cultivate positivity. It reflects the path I have traveled and the person I have become. I am forever grateful for God's love and guidance; they have been my constant companions in this beautiful life journey.

Relying on God was the only possibility I could ever do. As a young girl still learning about life, I developed an independent mindset by seeing the goodness in everything. My family faced numerous challenges growing up, but we always held onto our faith.

My parents were hardworking individuals who instilled in me the values of perseverance and determination. They were deeply religious and believed we could overcome obstacles with God's guidance. I witnessed their devotion firsthand as they relied on prayer and faith to navigate the ups and downs of life.

AMID MY QUESTIONABLE EXISTENCE

Amidst life's difficulties, my parents never lost hope. We faced our fair share of hardships, but my parents taught me that setbacks were merely opportunities in disguise. Instead of dwelling on our circumstances, they taught me to be grateful for what we had and trust God's plan.

As I grew older, I faced challenges of my own. Life was not always smooth sailing, but God had a purpose for everything. Through faith, I found the strength to overcome adversity and learn from my experiences.

In my teenage years, I became more involved in church activities. I discovered a passion for helping others and spreading love and kindness to those around me. My faith was a guiding light for me and those who crossed my path.

During my college years, I faced the daunting task of choosing a career path. It was a time filled with uncertainty and self-doubt. However, I turned to God for guidance, asking for a sign to lead me in the right direction. Through prayer, I found clarity and peace. I realized that my passion lay in serving others and positively impacting their lives. With unwavering faith, I pursued a career in social work, dedicating myself to helping the less fortunate and bringing about positive change.

***

Throughout my life, I have faced hardships, disappointments, and heartaches. However, my faith has always been my rock. It has given me the strength to persevere, the courage to face challenges head-on, and the wisdom to see the bigger picture.

Relying on God has taught me humility, empathy, and compassion. It has shaped my character and defined who I am today. My faith has guided me through the darkest times and has been a constant source of inspiration and hope.

As I reflect on my journey, I am grateful for the unwavering faith instilled in me by my parents. It has been my life's cornerstone and has given me the courage to pursue my dreams fearlessly.

In a chaotic and unpredictable world, relying on God has been my compass, guiding me through the darkest days and leading me toward a life of purpose and fulfillment. I am grateful for the lessons I've learned, the challenges I've overcome, and the unwavering faith that has shaped every aspect of my autobiography.

As a teenage girl growing up, I always struggled with self-doubt and a lack of confidence. I felt as though I was constantly being held back by my negative thoughts and limiting beliefs. No matter what I accomplished, I never felt truly satisfied or fulfilled. I knew that if I wanted to break free from this cycle, I needed to make a change.

One day, I came across a book that would forever alter the course of my life. It was called "The Power of Positive Thinking" by Norman Vincent Peale, "Think Big" by Ben Carson, M.D., and "The Magic of Thinking Big" by David J. Schwartz, Ph.D., Intrigued by the promise of a new mindset, I eagerly delved into its pages.

As I read the book, I realized how much my mindset held me back. I had always believed that success was reserved for those naturally talented or lucky. But Peale's words challenged this belief, urging me to take control of my thoughts and beliefs.

I realized that if I wanted to achieve my goals and live a fulfilling life, I needed to cultivate a mindset of positivity and abundance. I embraced the idea that my thoughts could shape my reality and that by choosing to think positively, I could attract success and happiness into my life.

With this newfound understanding, I embarked on a journey of self-transformation. I started by challenging my negative thoughts and replacing them with positive affirmations. Whenever a self-doubting thought crept into my mind, I countered it with a positive declaration reaffirming my abilities and potential.

It was challenging at first. I had spent so many years ingraining negative thought patterns into my mind that breaking free from them required consistent effort and dedication. But I pressed on, knowing the rewards would be well worth it.

I also surrounded myself with like-minded individuals who shared my desire for personal growth and development. Their positive energy and unwavering belief in me inspired and motivated me. We supported one another on our respective journeys, cheering each other on and celebrating our victories, no matter how small.

As I continued to nurture my new mindset, I noticed a significant shift in my life. Opportunities that I once believed were out of reach suddenly presented themselves. I found the courage to pursue my passions and chase after my dreams. Failure and setbacks no longer deterred me but served as valuable learning experiences and stepping stones toward success.

Today, I can confidently say that choosing and learning to have a new, profound mindset was one of the best decisions I've ever made. It has allowed me to break free from limiting beliefs, unlock my true potential, and create a life filled with purpose, joy, and abundance.

AMID MY QUESTIONABLE EXISTENCE

In sharing my journey, I inspire others to embark on their path of self-transformation. Every individual has the power to choose their mindset and shape their destiny. By embracing positivity, self-belief, and the power of our thoughts, we can overcome any obstacle and create the life we truly desire.

At a certain point in my life, after I decided to surrender my life to Jesus. This marked a turning point for me, as my mind and focus shifted towards the things of God. Each day became a fresh start, a chance for me to grow as a young woman in the eyes of all those around me.

I was no stranger to difficulties and challenges; they were the sacrifices I knew came with a life devoted to God. But little did I realize the actual depth of what awaited me. There were moments when it seemed like everything was falling apart when the world around me appeared chaotic and uncertain. In those moments, I clung to the grace of God, finding solace in the knowledge that He would always protect and shield me.

It was during these times of trial and tribulation that my faith was truly put to the test. I wrestled with doubt, struggled with fear, and questioned whether I had made the right choice. But in the depths of my uncertainty, I found that my faith only grew stronger. I learned to rely on God's promises, trusting He would never leave or forsake me.

As I journeyed on this path, I met countless individuals who shaped my spiritual growth. From wise mentors to fellow believers, they became my guiding lights, helping me navigate the challenges ahead. Their wisdom and encouragement reminded me that I was not alone on this journey and that others had faced similar trials and appeared more robust in their faith.

Through it all, I discovered the transformative power of prayer. It became my lifeline, a direct line of communication with the Creator of the universe. I poured out my heart in despair, seeking solace and guidance. Repeatedly, I saw the miraculous answers to my prayers as God faithfully showed up and provided for my every need.

Looking back on my journey, I am filled with awe and gratitude for how God has worked in my life. He has turned my brokenness into something beautiful, molding me into the woman He created me to be. I am no longer the person I once was, for His grace has transformed me from the inside out.

Though challenges still arise, I face them with newfound strength, knowing God's love and protection surround me. Surrendering my life to Jesus was the best decision ever, and I am eternally grateful for my faith journey. Each day is a reminder of His faithfulness, and I am encouraged to continue pressing forward, knowing that He who began a decent work in me will carry it on to completion.

I would encourage anyone facing difficulties or unsure of the path ahead to seek God wholeheartedly. Surrender your life to Him and trust in His plans for your future. He will be your constant source of strength and protection, guiding you through every season of life. As I have experienced firsthand, His grace is sufficient, and His love knows no bounds.

***

Reflection

From an early age, my parents instilled in me the values of hard work, compassion, and perseverance. As I navigated through the formative years of my life, a sense of self-awareness began to stir within me. Alongside the familiar comforts of home, I felt an unshakable yearning for something more profound.

As I matured, questions started to fill my mind. Who am I? What is my purpose? Why am I here? These existential inquiries persisted, compelling me to embark on a journey to search for my life's true calling and purpose here on Earth.

With determination in my heart and a sense of curiosity driving me forward, I set out on a path that would take me beyond the boundaries of my small town. I sought knowledge and experiences that would shed light on the mysteries of life and help me uncover the true meaning of my existence.

Leaving familiarity behind, I ventured into the world with an open mind and an eagerness to explore. I immersed myself in various cultures, interacting with people from diverse backgrounds and engaging in conversations that broadened my horizons.

AMID MY QUESTIONABLE EXISTENCE

Through encounters with individuals facing adversities and hardships, I discovered the immense power of compassion. Witnessing the resilience of those who faced unimaginable challenges, I realized the importance of helping those in need. This newfound understanding planted a seed of empathy within me, fueling my desire to make a positive impact on the lives of others.

I also explored my passions and talents as I delved deeper into understanding the world. I pursued education and pushed boundaries, acquiring knowledge that captivated my interest. I threw myself into various endeavors, from arts to sciences, uncovering hidden abilities and honing existing skills.

Yet, searching for my purpose was not without moments of doubt and uncertainty. There were times when the path seemed obscured, and I wondered if I would ever find the answers I sought. But in those moments, the values instilled in me during my upbringing reminded me to persevere.

With unwavering determination, I pressed on, recognizing that the journey itself held intrinsic value. It was about the destination, growth, self-discovery, and lessons learned. Step by step, I found myself slowly piecing together fragments of my purpose, like a puzzle forming its complete picture.

My path became more apparent through encounters with remarkable individuals, compassionate acts of service, and the pursuit of knowledge. I realized my calling was to inspire and uplift others – to catalyze positive change in the world.

Armed with this newfound understanding, I returned to my modest town, grateful for the love and support that had nurtured my journey thus far. Now, equipped with a purpose and a burning desire to make a difference, I dedicated myself to building a community where individuals could thrive, fostering an environment that embraced diversity, compassion, and growth.

My story is an ongoing, ever-evolving tale as I uncover more about myself and the world around me. The road ahead may be filled with challenges, but armed with the values instilled in me and the understanding of my purpose, I am ready to face them head-on and leave a legacy of love, compassion, and perseverance.

In my quest for meaning, I have discovered that life's purpose lies not in a static destination but in the journey itself – a journey of self-discovery, growth, and relentless pursuit of making a difference in the lives of others. As I reflect upon my life's journey thus far, I am grateful for the opportunity to embark on this remarkable adventure of finding my true calling and purpose here on Earth.

CHAPTER 9

UNEXPECTED EVENTS

It was 2022 when the tides of fate turned from right to left, forever altering the course of my family's life. We found ourselves uprooted from our familiar existence, compelled to leave behind our beloved residence at one of the Kips Bay Towers and seek refuge in one of the Brooklyn neighborhoods. Little did we know that this would mark the beginning of one of the most complex and trying times my family would ever experience.

The decision to move was a challenging one. We had established a comfortable life in the heart of New York City, and the thought of leaving it all behind was daunting and heart-wrenching. However, circumstances beyond our control forced us to make this difficult choice.

As we settled into a temporary home in Brooklyn, a sense of uncertainty loomed over us. The neighborhood was unfamiliar, and the change of scenery felt jarring. We had to adjust to the different rhythms of life, new faces, and a whole set of challenges ahead.

The distance from our friends and neighbors was one of the most significant adjustments. We had built strong connections at Kips Bay Towers, where we met new people. The sudden separation from this tight-knit community left us yearning for the familiar warmth and camaraderie that came with it.

Financially, the move also placed a strain on our resources. The cost of living in Brooklyn was higher than anticipated, and we had to reassess our budget and make sacrifices to make ends meet. It was a humbling experience for us, as we had to let go of certain luxuries and adjust to a more frugal way of life.

Furthermore, education has become a primary concern. My sisters and I had to adjust to the new commute to go to school. The process was stressful, but we were determined to ensure that our children's education did not suffer due to our circumstances.

The experience of uprooting our lives and starting anew taught us invaluable life lessons. It taught us to appreciate the small moments of joy, to cherish the bonds forged through adversity, and to embrace change with courage and grace.

Though our time at Kips Bay Towers will always hold a special place in our hearts, the unexpected twist of fate that led us to Brooklyn ultimately shaped our family in ways we could have never imagined. It is a chapter of our lives etched with both struggle and triumph, forever carving our story with resilience and the indomitable spirit that defines us. The once-familiar surroundings were replaced with an unfamiliar atmosphere filled with the echoes of despair and solitude. However, we were not alone in this challenge. Gratitude swelled within our hearts for those who stood by us in our time of need, offering their unwavering support and unyielding optimism.

Yet, indifference and betrayal emerged in the sea of compassion. People we had known for years turned their backs on us, their faces cold and impassive. It was disheartening to witness the transformation of individuals we once held dear as they revealed hidden aspects of their characters that we never anticipated. But through it all, we learned a profound lesson about the true nature of humanity. The harsh reality of life began to unveil itself before my eyes...

TO BE CONTINUE...

AMID MY QUESTIONABLE EXISTENCE

ABOUT THE AUTHOR

Rachel Tugutu was born and raised in Tanzania, deep in the heart of Africa. She developed a passion for music at a young age, listening to her parents singing traditional melodies. Her love for music grew, and she eventually began to write her songs. Rachel's music is unique because she draws inspiration from her African roots and modern events worldwide. She melds these two worlds together to create a unique sound. She combines modern styles of music and sensibilities with contemporary topics to create music that speaks to both young and old. Rachel's songs have the potential to reach and inspire people globally. She wants her music to reflect her Tanzanian heritage and the broader strife and struggle facing the world today. She also hopes her music will entertain and effectively spark meaningful conversations. Through her inspiring and empowering compositions, she's determined to take her talents to the world. And with the desire to empower and help people find solutions for a better future and spread the message of hope through her music.

AMID MY QUESTIONABLE EXISTENCE

TO GOD BE THE GLORY!!!

Printed in the USA
CPSIA information can be obtained
at www.ICGtesting.com
LVHW050615011224
797923LV00016B/821